Taste*ful*

NAOMI CRISANTE

Foreword **Gabriel Gaté**   Photography **Joshua Lynott**

For Domenic, who knows where life lives

Taste*ful*

Flavoursome food to share
with style at your table

Contents

Spring *flings* 12

Poached Eggs with Charred Corn and Avocado 16
Broad Bean and Basil Bruschetta 18
Tomato, Olive and Feta Puffs 21
Stuffed Zucchini Flowers with Basil Oil and Chilli 22
Pan-fried Haloumi with Chilli Cucumber Salsa 24
Roast Whole Snapper with Basil Tomatoes
  and Feta Pilaf 26
Garlicky Prawns with Chargrilled Toast 29
Saffron Fritto Misto with Roast Capsicum Aioli 32
Pizza Party 34
  - Mixed Olive Napoletana Pizza 37
  - Greek Lamb and Feta Pizza 37
  - Smoked Salmon, Brie and Caviar Pizza 37
  - Prawn and Chorizo Pizza 37
  - Duck, Fig and Rocket Pizza 37
  - Mortadella, Bocconcini and Pistachio Pizza 37
Cheat's Foccacia 37
Veal Saltimbocca with Caper Wine Sauce 39
Hazelnut and Fennel Pork Cutlets
  with Quick Corn Relish 41
Roast Pumpkin and Chorizo Paella 42
Artichoke and Olive Pissaladiére 45
Spiral Spanakopita 48
Radish, Pea and Rocket Salad 50
Smoky Chicken and Broccolini Orzo 53
Ratatouille Lamb 54
Southern Fried Chicken Fingers with Remoulade 56
Green Vegetable Salad with Dill Dijonnaise 58
Baby Cucumber Salad with Olives, Pine Nuts
  and Tomato Dressing 58

Summer *love* 60

Roast Tomato and Whipped Feta Bruschetta 64
King Prawn Pâté with Tortilla Crisps 67
Zucchini Dill Fritters with Brie and Plum Chutney 68
Spanish Orange and Fennel Salad 70
Charred Corn with Maple Butter 72
Grilled Sardines with Green Olive Salsa
  and Garlic Croutons 74
Red Wine Octopus with Feta Dressing 78
Summertime Fennel Mussels 78
Egyptian Fattoush Salad 81
Chargrilled Quail with Freekeh
  and Pomegranate Salad 83
Prawn, Pea and Pistachio Linguine 84
Sesame Eggplant Quinoa with
  Orange Tahini Dressing 87
Za'atar and Haloumi Lamb Cutlets
  with Esme Salad 91
Spice-rubbed Duck Legs with Roast Nectarines
  and Cherries 92
Sumac Chicken with Apple Mint Salad
  and Cranberries 94
Italian Veal with Tuna and Caper Sauce
  and Asparagus 97
Stuffed Zucchini Wrapped in Prosciutto 98
Slow-roasted Salmon with Salad Verde
  and Smoky Aioli 100
Minted Lamb Kofta with Beetroot Cacik 102
Buffalo Mozzarella with Nectarines, Honey
  and Petals 104

Foreword 6
Introduction 9
General tips for recipe success 10

Acknowledgements 204
When Naomi met Josh 206

Autumn *passions* 108

Magic Mushrooms on Toast 112

Roast Capsicum with Feta and Olives 114

Pistachio Crumbed Olives with Basil Mayo 117

Roast Beetroot and Radicchio with Balsamic Glaze 119

Sesame Carrots with Mandarin Juice 120

Kipfler Potato, Radish and Pea Salad 122

Cioppino Seafood Stew and Parmesan Garlic Rolls 126

Moroccan Chicken Pie (B'stilla) 128

Polenta-crumbed Flathead with Caper Mayonnaise on Garlic Mash 131

Persian Chicken Pilaf 132

Seared Duck Breast with Pinot Grapes and Duck Fat Potatoes 134

Eggplant Involtini with Tomato Capsicum Sauce 136

Swiss Brown Mushroom and Gruyère Tart 140

Homemade Gnocchi with Wild Mushroom Sauce 142

Chicken, Chorizo and Sundried Tomato Risotto 145

Turkish Lamb Pide 146

Roast Pumpkin Rotolo 148

Gruyère Chicken with French Onion Sauce and Paris Mash 150

Chicken Scaloppine with Marsala Mushrooms and Soft Polenta 152

Mighty Muffuletta 155

Winter *comforts* 156

Hot Parmesan and Artichoke Dip with Sesame Cumin Crisps 160

Feta Cigars with Mandarin and Thyme Honey 163

Cannellini Crostini 164

Mussel, Celery and Potato Chowder with Mustard Toasts 166

Moroccan Chicken, Lentil and Spinach Soup with Coriander Oil 169

Skillet Eggplant Parmigiana 170

Poulet au Pot 175

Seafood Chowder Pies 176

Prosciutto and Porcini Beef Fillet 179

Shiraz Beef Cheeks with Parsnip Pear Puree 181

Moroccan Tagine with Flatbreads 182

Mimi's Moussaka 185

Lamb Shank Navarin and Ploughman's Cheese Bread 188

Rosemary Beef Short Ribs with Sweet Pea Puree 190

Surprise Mozzarella Meatballs 192

Bourbon Beef Brisket with Quickles and Celeriac Slaw 194

Rigatoni with Italian Sausage and Spinach Ragù 197

Slow-cooked Pork, Spinach and Cannellini Bean Pot Roast with Salt-roasted Chats 198

Giant Pumpkin and Bacon Pie 200

Honeyed Brussels Sprouts with Almond and Dijon Dressing 203

 Check out Naomi's seasonal playlists to match each chapter of recipes for the complete experience! Turn to p208 for the QR codes.

Foreword

About 30 years ago I observed a charismatic young woman skilfully demonstrating recipes to a captive audience at the popular Gas and Fuel Cooking School in foodie Melbourne. What struck me at the time was how relaxed this charming cookery teacher was whilst encouraging a friendly interaction between her students and herself.

It was obvious for me that Naomi Zouliou, as she was then known, had a talent for food and cooking which she inherited from her food-loving parents, both of Greek heritage. Naomi's Dad was brought up in multicultural Egypt and her Mum in stunning Romania. Interestingly, Naomi's husband, Domenic Crisante, is of Italian descent.

Naomi learned her cooking and teaching skills at RMIT in the legendary Emily McPherson building that trained so many outstanding domestic science teachers. Over the years she became a much appreciated food communicator and influencer, appearing in many television programs, developing recipes, styling food, speaking on radio and writing for newspapers and magazines.

Naomi and I have been friends for many years and have worked together on various projects, starting with her appearance on my television show, *What's Cooking?* in the early nineties.

Now Naomi is the author of this beautiful family and special occasion cookbook. The well-written recipes in *Tasteful* have a strong Mediterranean and Middle Eastern flavour reflecting her wide experience as a professional and understanding of the challenges of being a happy home cook.

Beautifully illustrated, this handsome book is full of practical cooking tips as well as wine suggestions to match with the food. Photographer Josh Lynott has created stunning images of the delicious dishes. So please, make yourself comfortable, open Naomi's book and allow yourself to be transported to a world of beautiful food that will inspire you in your future cooking adventures.

Gabriel Gaté

Introduction

I remember the moment when I first became a good cook. I was 14 and had made boeuf bourguignon – a rich, slowly simmered wonder that filled the senses with its deep flavours and warm aroma. Setting it on the table for my family filled me with pride in the joy and shared experience I had created for them.

This is the heart of my cooking to this day: to give people pleasure and inspire them to do the same for others.

Food is such a sensory experience. At its most basic, it nourishes and satiates us. At its best, it can bond people and create long-lasting memories. When we share food, it connects us, much like the breaking of bread. That's why my dishes are made for sharing at the table.

These recipes have developed over my lifetime. They are the meals I have served my family and friends and taught to my students.

During COVID-19 lockdown, my group of regular Cook-Along-ers would Zoom into my kitchen to cook step-by-step with me, before enjoying dinner with their families and loved ones. We explored new dishes, cuisines and techniques, and their enthusiasm, feedback and love of my style of food gave me the confidence to finally write this book.

As you cook through the seasons as I love to do, you'll experience a variety of flavours, techniques and presentations, in both familiar and new dishes.

My food style is deeply rooted in my Mediterranean heritage, travels, studies, and my professional experience. The flavours of Greece, Italy, France, Spain, Morocco, Egypt, Lebanon and Turkey excite me, and I love experimenting with them.

As a food stylist, recipe developer, teacher and presenter for over 35 years, I have made a career of communicating about food and creating good cooks. My recipes are designed so you can achieve success at home, and always feature a little 'Naomi twist'.

When I asked my students why they liked my recipes, their responses were, "They taste so good", "They are always delicious", "I love how taste-full they are" … and so, Tasteful was born. It describes not only my food, but how it is served and presented and, most importantly, how I like to live.

I hope you enjoy these flavoursome recipes and that you too will be applauded for good-looking and great-tasting food served with style at your own table.

Enjoy!

Naomi x

General tips for recipe success

These tips will help you achieve success with my recipes:

- The book is arranged in seasons and each recipe is marked as a Starter, Main, Side, Snack or Salad as a serving suggestion.
- Please read the recipe in its entirety before commencing cooking.
- Preparation time stated does not include the cooking time, which is separate.
- Check you have all the required ingredients and equipment beforehand.
- Use Australian standard measuring cups and spoons.
- Measure ingredients and prepare them as listed in the ingredients as part of your 'mise en place' (preparation) before cooking.
- Most of the sub-recipes denoted in bold in the method can be done in advance.
- All oven temperatures are conventional unless stated. Drop temperature by 10°C if using a fan-forced oven.
- Always preheat the oven to the stated temperature before cooking.
- A handheld blender and a jug are suitable for most recipes requiring blending.
- A French oven is a heavy-based pot usually made from enamel-coated cast iron that can be used for the stovetop or oven.
- Grill refers to browning under an overhead grill. Chargrill refers to cooking on a chargrill or griddle pan.
- Use 60g or 70g eggs (700g/800g cartons).
- Butter is salted unless otherwise specified.
- Extra virgin olive oil is widely used for most recipes, with pure olive oil for general use and extra light olive oil for frying or a lighter taste.
- Spring onions are also known as green onions, green shallots or scallions. Golden shallots are also known as eschalots or French shallots.
- Use sea salt and freshly ground black pepper for best flavour.
- Plastic wrap, foil, baking paper, kitchen twine and muslin are good to have on hand.
- Asterisks* have been used in recipes to reference extra information.
- Variations are included in most recipes, as well as vegetarian options.
- You will find tips and styling guidance at the bottom of each recipe.
- Drink matches, including wine, beer and spirits, have been recommended for each dish.
- For recipes that call for wine, use the wine you are planning to serve with the dish so the flavours complement.

This book is also interactive. Discover more.

GENERAL TIPS FOR RECIPE SUCCESS 11

Spring
flings

The sparkle of Spring is like a twinkle in the eye.

It's time to throw off the heaviness for lighter fare with a spring in its step.

Lift the mood with brightness, crunch and bursts of freshness that call us back out into the cool air towards those glimmering rays.

SPRING FLINGS

Breakfast
Poached Eggs with Charred Corn and Avocado

Serves 4 • **Preparation time** 15 minutes • **Cooking time** 10 minutes

You don't need to go out for brekkie when you can rustle up something as tasty as this and when the yolk is just right, it's a great start to the morning. I am lucky that my hubby is an excellent egg poacher, he has more patience than me!

400g can corn kernels, drained
1 avocado, finely diced
1 large ripe tomato, finely diced
2 spring onions, chopped
2 tablespoons chopped coriander or parsley
1 lime, cut into quarters
sea salt and pepper, to taste
4 or 8 eggs
sriracha mayonnaise, for drizzling
smoked paprika or chilli powder, for sprinkling
toast, for serving

Place the corn in a flat layer in an oiled pan and cook over high heat for 5 minutes until the corn chars.

Combine avocado, tomato, spring onions and coriander together. Squeeze a little of each lime wedge into the avocado mix, keeping the wedges for serving. Season.

Poach the eggs* to your liking.

Arrange the corn in the middle of the plate. Spoon the avocado mixture in the centre. Top with a poached egg or two, drizzle with sriracha mayonnaise and serve sprinkled with paprika and a lime wedge on the side. Serve with toast.

VARIATION The corn and avocado mixture is delicious on toast spread with goat's cheese for those who don't eat eggs.

*To poach eggs: use a deep saucepan of boiling water and add at least 1 tablespoon vinegar. Break egg into a small bowl. Reduce water to a simmer and swirl before gently lowering the egg into the centre of the whirlpool. Simmer for 2-3 minutes until done to your liking. Remove with a slotted spoon and drain on absorbent paper or a spare piece of bread.

TIPS
You can make your own sriracha mayonnaise by mixing 1 cup egg mayonnaise with 2 tablespoons sriracha chilli sauce.

STYLING
Swirl the sriracha mayonnaise around the edge of the plate as a finishing touch.

DRINK MATCH
Sparkling, mimosa, fresh juice, or fruited sour ale.

Brunch/Starter

Broad Bean and Basil Bruschetta

Serves 4 • **Preparation time** 15 minutes • **Cooking time** 15 minutes

Time to graduate from smashing avocados to mashing broad beans. These creamy green beans are just beautiful for a brunch bruschetta.

250g shelled fresh broad beans
1 clove garlic, crushed
extra virgin olive oil
sea salt and pepper, to taste
lemon juice, to taste
½ cup basil leaves
4 slices ciabatta or crusty bread
50g soft goat's cheese or mashed feta
chopped pistachios or toasted pine nuts, for garnish

Boil broad beans in salted water for 10 minutes. Drain and refresh under cold water. Remove the skins, using a small knife to nick one end, and pop out the inner bean. Mash with garlic, ¼ cup olive oil and season to taste with lemon juice and salt. Chop half the basil and mix in.

Brush bread with olive oil and grill on both sides until toasted. Spread with goat's cheese and top with broad bean mixture. Drizzle with olive oil and serve sprinkled with pistachios, pepper and remaining basil leaves.

VARIATION Also delicious topped with some crispy fried prosciutto.

TIPS
Look out for fresh broad beans when they are in season in the spring; otherwise, frozen broad beans are a great standby.

STYLING
Keep aside the tiniest basil leaves for garnish.

DRINK MATCH
Sauvignon blanc, cider or Japanese rice lager.

Starter
Tomato, Olive and Feta Puffs

Makes 32 • **Preparation time** 10 minutes • **Cooking time** 10 minutes

These quick-as-a-flash pastries are the perfect pass-around and I always keep butter puff pastry sheets in my freezer for this reason. A tasty little trio of tomato, olives and feta give these a definite Greek twist and they are particularly good with a shot of ouzo on ice.

350g marinated feta in oil
2 frozen butter puff pastry sheets, thawed
16 cherry tomatoes, halved
32 pitted black olives

Drain marinated feta, reserving oil. Prick puff pastry lightly with a fork, cut each sheet into 16 squares and place on oven trays lined with baking paper.

Top each square with a cube of marinated feta, a tomato half and an olive.

Bake at 230°C for 5-8 minutes until puffed and golden. Drizzle each puff with a little of the oil from the feta and serve immediately.

VARIATIONS Here are some other easy topping ideas to try:
- Tomato and anchovy
- Pesto and olive
- Roast capsicum and feta
- Goat's cheese, tuna and capers
- Blue cheese, walnut and quince paste

TIPS
Puffs can be assembled and refrigerated until ready to be baked, up to 4 hours in advance.

STYLING
Drizzle with herbed oil just before serving.

DRINK MATCH
Sparkling pinot noir, ouzo on ice or crisp lager.

SPRING FLINGS

Starter

Stuffed Zucchini Flowers with Basil Oil and Chilli

Makes 8 • **Preparation time** 30 minutes • **Cooking time** 10 minutes

When I see zucchini flowers appear in the garden, I just have to have them. Unfurling the blossom to fill it with a surprise centre is such a satisfying thing. They are then dipped in a simple beer batter and fried to crispness, just before serving with basil oil and chilli sauce.

1 cup basil leaves
⅓ cup extra virgin olive oil
sea salt and pepper, to taste
125g fresh full-fat ricotta, cut from the wheel
50g grated parmesan
8 zucchini flowers
½ cup beer
½ cup self-raising flour
extra light olive oil, for deep-frying
sriracha chilli sauce, for serving
basil leaves, for garnish

Blend basil, extra virgin olive oil and ½ teaspoon salt to a paste.

Combine ricotta and parmesan and season to taste. Carefully remove the centre pistil from each flower and fill with ricotta mixture, closing the bloom around the cheese.

Just prior to cooking, whisk beer into flour to make a batter. Thinly coat each flower completely in batter and deep fry in hot extra light olive oil until golden. Drain on absorbent paper.

Dollop serving plates with basil oil and small drops of chilli sauce and serve stuffed zucchini flowers on top. Garnish with basil leaves.

VARIATION Marinated feta can be used in place of ricotta and parmesan, and make use of the feta's marinating oil in the basil oil.

TIPS
Use soda water in place of beer if you prefer.

STYLING
Spoon little pools of basil oil onto the plate and position the zucchini flowers on top, then squeeze drops of chilli sauce in between before finishing with basil leaves.

DRINK MATCH
Sparkling, pinot grigio or crisp lager.

Starter

Pan-fried Haloumi with Chilli Cucumber Salsa

Serves 6 • **Preparation time** 10 minutes • **Cooking time** 5 minutes

Haloumi, a 'squeaky' Cypriot-style stretched cheese, turns crusty golden on the outside and softer in the middle when quickly seared in a hot pan. I love serving it piping hot on little toasted pieces of Turkish bread as a pass-around, topped with a crunchy cucumber salsa to contrast flavours.

1 Lebanese cucumber, finely diced
¼ cup coriander leaves
sweet chilli sauce
2 teaspoons lime or lemon juice
sea salt and pepper, to taste
12 slices Turkish bread
180g haloumi, drained

Combine cucumber, coriander, 2 tablespoons sweet chilli sauce and lime juice together and season to taste. Toast bread slices until golden. Cut haloumi into 12 slices.

Just prior to serving, heat an oiled pan and pan fry haloumi for 1-2 minutes until golden on both sides.

Serve immediately on toasted bread topped with Chilli Cucumber Salsa and drizzled with sweet chilli sauce.

VARIATION Replace haloumi with sliced tofu coated in polenta and pan fried in an oiled pan for a vegan option.

TIPS
For a delicious salad, combine rocket with cucumber salsa, top with pan-fried haloumi and dress with light olive oil and lime juice.

STYLING
Chargrill the pieces of toast so they have grill marks on them. Add a little drizzle of sweet chilli sauce and a sprinkle of coriander leaves to garnish.

DRINK MATCH
Riesling or XPA.

Main

Roast Whole Snapper with Basil Tomatoes and Feta Pilaf

Serves 4 • Preparation time 15 minutes • Cooking time 30-40 minutes

My mum always used to bake snapper with tomatoes, Greek-style. They certainly give the meatiness of snapper a Mediterranean edge, particularly when finished with tender basil leaves.

4 spring onions, chopped
3 cloves garlic, crushed
1 teaspoon fennel seeds
sea salt and pepper, to taste
2 tablespoons extra virgin olive oil
1-1.2kg cleaned whole snapper or barramundi
1 punnet cherry tomatoes, halved, or 3 large ripe tomatoes, diced
1 tablespoon capers
½ bunch fresh basil leaves

FETA PILAF
50g butter
1 tablespoon olive oil
2 cups long grain rice
1 litre chicken stock
200g feta cheese, crumbled

Combine spring onions, garlic, fennel seeds, 1 teaspoon salt and oil together. Cut three slashes into each side of the snapper and place on a roasting tray. Fill each cavity with 2 tablespoons of spring onion mixture. Add tomatoes and capers to remaining spring onion mixture and arrange over and around snapper. Season.

Roast at 200°C for 30-40 minutes until fish is just cooked. Remove fish onto a serving platter and cover to keep warm. Transfer tomatoes into a bowl, allow to cool slightly, stir in basil leaves and spoon over fish for serving. Serve with Feta Pilaf.

To make **Feta Pilaf**, heat butter and oil in a large saucepan until melted. Add rice and cook until opaque and lightly toasted. Heat stock, add to the rice, bring to the boil and simmer covered over low heat for 10 minutes. Do not remove lid. Turn off heat and stand covered for 10 minutes. Fluff with a fork, stir in feta and serve with fish.

VARIATION Whole small rainbow trout can be used in place of the snapper and served as individual portions.

TIPS
To portion fish, use a large flat spoon to release flesh from the bones on one side, remove head and skeleton, and portion the rest.

STYLING
Keep some fresh basil leaves and capers for sprinkling. Use a basil leaf to discretely cover the eye!

DRINK MATCH
Pinot noir or saison.

SPRING FLINGS

Starter/Main

Garlicky Prawns with Chargrilled Toast

Serves 4 • **Preparation time** 15 minutes • **Cooking time** 10 minutes

Fast food at its best, a pan of prawns tossed in garlicky butter and finished with smoked paprika is my favourite Spanish tapas-style dish. The charred pieces of toast are there for good looks and great dipping.

1 baguette, cut into diagonal slices
extra virgin olive oil, for brushing
smoked paprika, for sprinkling
100g butter
8 cloves garlic, crushed
500g peeled green prawns, deveined
2 tablespoons chopped continental parsley
sea salt and pepper, to taste
lemon wedges, for serving

Brush baguette slices with oil then chargrill or grill on both sides and sprinkle with smoked paprika.

Melt butter and garlic together in a large frypan and sauté for 1 minute. Add prawns and sauté for a few minutes until the prawns are just cooked. Stir in parsley, sprinkle with smoked paprika and season to taste.

Serve with lemon wedges and chargrilled bread to mop up the garlic butter.

VARIATION Try with scallops instead of prawns or use a mixture of the two.

TIPS
As soon as the prawns turn pink, remove from the heat so they don't overcook.

STYLING
Cook in a cast iron pan and serve it hot at the table with a final sprinkle of parsley and paprika.

DRINK MATCH
Albarino, vermouth or German pilsner.

SPRING FLINGS

Starter/Main

Saffron Fritto Misto with Roast Capsicum Aioli

Serves 4-6 • **Preparation time** 30 minutes • **Cooking time** 30 minutes

The fish markets of Venice inspired this dish for me. Crisp saffron-battered bites of seafood and vegetables with a punchy capsicum aioli make an impressive share platter. My crunchy tempura-style batter is a little more Japanese in texture, so the food is just lightly coated to show off its shape.

500g baby squid, baby octopus or calamari rings
500g green prawn cutlets
500g cleaned sardines, sardine fillets or fish pieces
2 lemons
500g assorted vegetable pieces**
½ teaspoon saffron threads
extra light olive oil, for deep-frying
1¼ cups plain flour
½ cup cornflour
1 teaspoon baking powder
½ teaspoon salt
1½ cups chilled soda water
dill sprigs and sea salt flakes, for sprinkling

ROAST CAPSICUM AIOLI
1 large egg
4 cloves garlic, peeled
1 tablespoon lemon juice
1 teaspoon salt
1 teaspoon sugar
½ cup extra light olive oil
½ cup extra virgin olive oil
1 roast capsicum, peeled and seeded

Remove seafood from fridge. Finely slice 1 lemon and cut the second one into wedges. Prepare vegetables and make Roast Capsicum Aioli*. Soak saffron in 1 tablespoon boiling water.

Just before serving, heat oil in a wok or deep saucepan. Whisk flour, cornflour, baking powder and salt together in a bowl and stir in saffron water and freshly opened soda water to make a batter.

Working in batches, lightly dip vegetables, lemon slices and seafood into batter and deep fry until golden. Use a slotted spoon to remove any bits of batter from the oil. Drain on a paper towel-lined oven tray and keep warm in the oven as you cook batches. Serve with Roast Capsicum Aioli and lemon wedges.

For the ***Roast Capsicum Aioli**, combine egg, garlic, lemon juice, salt and sugar in a tall jug. Add extra light olive oil. Blend with a handheld blender, tilting the blender until smooth. Gradually stream in the extra virgin olive oil and continue blending until a thick mayonnaise is formed. Add capsicum and blend until smooth. Season to taste. Refrigerate for at least an hour for the garlic flavour to soften.

TIPS
**Use asparagus spears, green beans, broccolini, onion rings, slices of fennel or pumpkin, cauliflower florets etc.

STYLING
Best served on a large platter so you can see the shape of each piece. Finish with little sprigs of dill and sea salt flakes.

DRINK MATCH
Prosecco, pinot grigio or Australian pale ale.

Main
Pizza Party

Makes 6 pizzas (25cm round) • **Preparation time** 20 minutes (plus 2-4 hours proving time)
Cooking time 30 minutes

Nothing is quite as fun as making your own home-made pizzas. Here is my favourite no-knead pizza dough that produces a thin crispy base, and my suggested free-wheeling toppings to make you feel like you are in Napoli.

1kg bakers flour
5 teaspoons dried yeast (2 x 7g sachets)
1½ teaspoons salt
2 teaspoons sugar
3 cups warm water
extra virgin olive oil, as needed

Combine flour, yeast, salt and sugar in a large bowl. Make a well in the centre and mix in water and 1 tablespoon oil to make a sticky dough, no need to knead. Cover and allow to stand in a warm place for 2-4 hours until doubled in volume.

Grease pizza or oven trays with 2 tablespoons olive oil on each.

Using a plastic scraper, divide dough into six and place onto trays, working one at at time as needed. Using oiled hands, thinly press out and stretch dough onto trays, patting out and closing any holes. Allow to stand for 5 minutes.

Top with topping of choice and bake up to 2 pizzas at a time at 230°C for 20-30 minutes until golden. Use the pizza setting if your oven has one; otherwise, monitor the pizza, rotating in the oven to colour the base and top as required.

NOTE We cook our pizzas on a pizza stone in the smoker barbecue or covered charcoal barbecue and get great results.

TIPS
Bases can be par-baked with a little tomato passata and frozen for later use.

STYLING
Use pizza boards to pass the cut pizza around.

DRINK MATCH
Sangiovese or American pale ale.

Pizza Party *Continued*

These are flavoursome combinations that suit the party mood. Stretch the dough onto trays and organise ingredients in advance. Handwritten signs can also be helpful, and then the fun begins when guests can choose.

Mixed Olive Napoletana Pizza

Bake pizza base with tomato passata, grated mozzarella, mixed marinated olives and tiny cherry tomatoes. Finish with basil leaves.

Greek Lamb and Feta Pizza

Bake pizza base with tomato passata, crumbled feta and olives. Marinate 1 lamb backstrap in lemon, garlic, oregano and lemon juice and olive oil. Chargrill to medium rare and slice. Top pizza with spinach leaves, lamb, feta and extra olives. Finish with lemon, oregano and olive oil. For a vegetarian option, use chargrilled marinated eggplant slices in place of lamb.

Smoked Salmon, Brie and Caviar Pizza

Bake pizza base spread with garlic, olive oil and dill, and grated mozzarella. Top with brie slices, smoked salmon, salmon caviar and dill. Finish with lemon and pepper.

Prawn and Chorizo Pizza

Bake pizza base with tomato passata, grated mozzarella and sliced chorizo until golden. Top with green prawn cutlets marinated with chilli, lime and coriander and bake until prawns are cooked. Finish with coriander, lime and smoked paprika.

Duck, Fig and Rocket Pizza

Bake pizza base with caramelised onion and grated mozzarella. Top with cooked duck breast slices, pan-fried figs, rocket, toasted pine nuts, olive oil and balsamic glaze.

Mortadella, Bocconcini and Pistachio Pizza

Bake pizza base with grated mozzarella until golden. Top with mortadella and bake until a little golden. Top with torn bocconcini, slow roasted cherry tomatoes and pistachio pesto (blend ½ cup pistachios with 1 clove garlic, ⅓ cup extra virgin olive oil and ½ teaspoon salt).

Cheat's Focaccia

One quantity of dough will make 4 rectangular focaccia-style pizzas (30cm x 25 cm). Grease oven trays with ¼ cup extra virgin olive oil per tray. Divide dough into 4 and stretch each piece onto trays. Allow to stand for at least an hour to rise. Use your fingers to dimple the dough, drizzle liberally with oil and sprinkle with your topping of choice – olives, cherry tomatoes, onion/garlic, herbs etc – and sea salt.

Main

Veal Saltimbocca with Caper Wine Sauce

Serves 4 • **Preparation time** 15 minutes • **Cooking time** 15 minutes

A Roman favourite, saltimbocca literally means 'jump in the mouth', and these tasty morsels of veal certainly live up to their name. Perfect with a glass of pinot grigio.

800g veal escalopes
8 slices prosciutto
sea salt and pepper, to taste
1 bunch sage leaves
½ cup plain flour
50g butter
olive oil, as needed
3 cloves garlic, crushed
1 cup dry white wine
2 teaspoons baby capers
50g butter, cubed, extra
continental parsley, for garnish

Batten out veal escalopes between plastic wrap to 0.5cm thickness. Cut into pieces similar in size to prosciutto slices. Lay each piece on a slice of prosciutto, season and place 2 sage leaves in the centre. Fold in sides to enclose, making a parcel. Batten again lightly to seal. Coat in flour, pressing with your hand to flatten slightly.

Heat butter and 2 tablespoons oil in a large frypan. Add the veal and brown for 3-4 minutes on each side over high heat, until golden brown and cooked but still pink in the centre. Remove and keep warm. Wipe out pan.

Heat 1 tablespoon oil and sauté garlic until softened. Deglaze with wine, add capers and simmer until reduced and syrupy. Turn off heat and stir in extra butter to form a sauce. Serve over veal. Garnish with parsley leaves and pepper.

VARIATION Thin slices of pounded chicken fillet can be used in place of veal. Be sure to cook the chicken all the way through.

TIPS
Use a rolling pin or the flat side of a meat mallet to batten out the veal.

STYLING
Serve on a bed of steamed green beans and cherry tomatoes with calyxes. Add some fried sage leaves for extra garnish.

DRINK MATCH
Pinot grigio or Italian pilsner.

Main

Hazelnut and Fennel Pork Cutlets with Quick Corn Relish

Serves 4 • **Preparation time 15 minutes** • **Cooking time 15 minutes**

Whether it's cotoletta or schnitzel, I'm a sucker for crumbed meat and crumbed cutlets in particular. My favourite bit is nibbling the bone after! Here, juicy pork cutlets get a makeover with a hazelnut and fennel crumb and a cheat's corn relish on the side.

2 cups fresh or panko breadcrumbs
⅓ cup chopped hazelnuts
1 tablespoon fennel seeds
1 tablespoon chopped thyme
1 teaspoon salt
4 large pork cutlets
seasoned flour, for coating
1 large egg, lightly beaten
extra light olive oil or canola oil, for shallow frying
lemon wedges, for serving

QUICK CORN RELISH
1 cup canned corn kernels
2 spring onions, chopped
⅓ cup sweet chilli sauce
2 teaspoons lemon juice

Combine breadcrumbs, hazelnuts, fennel seeds, thyme and salt together. Coat pork cutlets in seasoned flour, dip in egg and coat in crumb mixture. Allow to stand on a wire rack for 5-10 minutes for crumbs to set.

Just prior to serving, shallow fry on both sides in hot oil until golden. Drain on an oven tray lined with absorbent paper. Remove the paper and bake at 200°C for 5-10 minutes to finish cooking. The pork is best served a little pink.

Serve with Quick Corn Relish, lemon wedges and salad.

For the **Quick Corn Relish**, use a fork to slightly crush the corn kernels and mix in remaining ingredients. Serve with pork.

VARIATION Use lamb cutlets in place of pork.

TIPS
Cutlets can be crumbed and kept refrigerated for up to 24 hours.

STYLING
Stack the cutlets on top of each other for serving and top with a little relish and thyme. Garnish with hazelnuts.

DRINK MATCH
Chardonnay, apple or pear cider.

Main

Roast Pumpkin and Chorizo Paella

Serves 4-6 • **Preparation time** 15 minutes • **Cooking time** 30 minutes

In my travels throughout Spain, I tried many a paella, from the traditional rabbit and green bean paella of Valencia to the paella mixta favoured by the tourists in Barcelona. There is much debate as to what is authentic but I have seen so many varieties that I think it's safe to submit my own.

600g pumpkin, peeled and cut into 2cm chunks
olive oil, as needed
sea salt, to taste
1 litre chicken or vegetable stock
¼ teaspoon saffron threads
1 red onion, sliced
1 yellow or red capsicum, cut into strips
2 Spanish-style chorizo sausages (soft not dried), sliced
1½ cups paella rice
2 teaspoons smoked paprika
coriander or continental parsley leaves, for garnish

Place pumpkin in paella pan. Drizzle with oil, season with salt and toss until coated. Roast at 200°C for 15 minutes until lightly browned, remove from pan and set aside. Bring stock and saffron to the boil while covered, then turn off heat and allow to infuse.

Place pan on stovetop and heat 1 tablespoon oil. Add onions, capsicum and chorizo and sauté until golden brown. Add rice and paprika and sauté for 2 minutes until rice is toasted. Stir in stock and place pumpkin pieces into rice. Simmer for 25-30 minutes, without stirring, until rice is cooked and a crust (socarrat) has formed underneath. You may need to add extra stock or water as needed.

Cover and stand for 5 minutes to cook completely. Serve sprinkled with extra paprika and coriander.

Scrape the socarrat crust off the base of the paella with a spoon and stir through the paella before serving.

VARIATION Use 250g halved Swiss brown mushrooms in place of chorizo and use vegetable stock for a vegan option.

TIPS
Use paella rice like Bomba or Calasparra for best results.

STYLING
Tease the top of the finished paella with a fork and finish with a generous sprinkle of smoked paprika and coriander leaves.

DRINK MATCH
Tempranillo, sangria or crisp lager.

Main/Snack

Artichoke and Olive Pissaladiére

Makes 1 x 30cm tart • **Preparation time** 30 minutes • **Cooking time** 30 minutes

Where Provence in France meets Liguria in Italy, this delightful hybrid of a tart and pizza was born. I first enjoyed it in Nice, and have added my own touch, the beautiful addition of flower-like artichokes and thyme to the onions, olives and anchovies. This is ideal picnic food as it doesn't need to be refrigerated and it transports well.

4 large onions, peeled
100g butter
½ bunch fresh thyme
2 sheets frozen butter puff pastry, thawed
2 x 45g tins anchovy fillets
6-8 small artichoke hearts (280g jar), cut in half
½ cup whole black olives

Finely slice the onions - use a mandolin if available. Place butter and onions in a large frypan and cook over medium-low heat for 30 minutes, stirring occasionally, until very soft and caramelised. Mix in 1 tablespoon chopped thyme. Allow to cool slightly.

Place puff pastry sheets on top of each other on a baking tray, score a 1cm border around the edges and prick the entire sheet with a fork. Spread caramelised onions onto the base of the pastry, within the border. Arrange the anchovies on top in a diamond lattice pattern. Decorate with artichoke halves and olives.

Bake at 200°C for 20 minutes until puffed and golden. If required, move the tray to the base of the oven to crisp the underneath for the last 5-10 minutes. Serve sprinkled with fresh thyme sprigs.

VARIATION Artichokes can be swapped out for stuffed green olives or cherry tomato halves.

TIPS
Always thaw frozen puff pastry sheets in the fridge for 15 minutes to minimise sweating.

STYLING
Serve whole at the table for best presentation.

DRINK MATCH
Pinot gris or American pale ale.

SPRING FLINGS

Main
Spiral Spanakopita

Serves 4-6 • **Preparation time** 20 minutes • **Cooking time** 25 minutes

My mum comes from a region of Greece that is known for their 'pites' - the spinach or vegetable pies made with hand-rolled filo. Mum taught herself to make it at 15, after her mother died in childbirth leaving behind her baby sister. As the woman of the house, she quickly learned how to cook for the family. I think the day she presented her father with her completed spanakopita and he kissed her hands in gratitude was the day she became a cook. My spiral spanakopita is an easier version that uses tissue-thin store-bought filo, but it is always a beautiful thing to bring to the table. I always feel the love in that moment.

250g spinach leaves
2 spring onions, chopped
½ cup chopped dill
½ teaspoon salt
200g feta cheese
2 eggs
16 sheets filo pastry
150g butter, melted
2 teaspoons sesame seeds or poppy seeds

Combine spinach, spring onions, dill and salt in a large bowl and squeeze together with your hands to bruise and soften leaves.

Crumble in feta cheese and mix in eggs.

Working quickly, brush one sheet of pastry with butter, top with a second sheet, brush with butter and spoon ⅛ of the filling along one of the long sides. Roll up tightly into a thin long roll, and spiral into the centre of a 30cm pizza tray or similar pan. Repeat with remaining mixture and pastry, inserting one end into the other as you add each new roll to the spiral. Brush liberally with butter and sprinkle with seeds.

Bake at 200°C for 20-25 minutes until puffed and golden. Position at the base of the oven for the last 5 minutes to crisp the base.

VARIATION Use grated zucchini or grated pumpkin in place of spinach. Parsley, chives or coriander can be used in place of dill.

TIPS
Use a damp tea towel to cover the filo pastry and prevent it drying out while you are working with it. Wrap unused pastry in plastic wrap and refrigerate for another use.

STYLING
You can also make 4 small individual spirals using two pastry rolls for each.

DRINK MATCH
Riesling or Australian pale ale.

SPRING FLINGS

Salad/Side

Radish, Pea and Rocket Salad

Serves 4 • **Preparation time** 15 minutes

The French know how to make the best of the humble radish, serving them simply with butter and sea salt. Their peppery crunch and pink brightness make for a great salad addition and a few sweet peas thrown in are a lovely contrast.

1 small red onion
2 tablespoons red wine vinegar
¼ teaspoon salt
½ teaspoon sugar
80g wild rocket
extra virgin olive oil, for drizzling
1 bunch radishes, finely sliced
¼ cup frozen green peas, thawed
2 tablespoons fresh mint leaves
1 teaspoon toasted fennel seeds

Finely slice the onion into thin rings. Combine with vinegar, salt and sugar, and allow to stand for 10 minutes.

Lightly dress rocket with olive oil and arrange on a serving platter.

Layer with radishes, peas, onion and mint leaves, then pour the vinegar dressing over the salad.

Drizzle with olive oil and serve sprinkled with fennel seeds.

VARIATION Add a little goat's cheese to the salad.

TIPS
To toast fennel seeds, dry fry in a pan until they are aromatic.

STYLING
Keep a little of the green tops on the radishes and slice thinly lengthwise to feature the green.

DRINK MATCH
Sauvignon blanc, rosé or fruited sour ale.

SPRING FLINGS 51

Main/Salad

Smoky Chicken and Broccolini Orzo

Serves 4 • **Preparation time** 20 minutes • **Cooking time** 15 minutes

Orzo pasta makes a delightful base for a salad. Here I have combined it with the unusual blend of broccolini, coriander and ruby grapefruit and topped it with easy-to-do smoky chicken slices. With its sweet and sour dressing, it works as an accompaniment or a meal in itself.

1 cup orzo or risoni pasta
sea salt and pepper, to taste
1 bunch coriander
2 large skinless chicken fillets
1 tablespoon smoked paprika
2 teaspoons dried thyme
extra virgin olive oil, as needed
2 spring onions, chopped
1 bunch broccolini, chopped
¼ cup toasted slivered almonds
1 ruby grapefruit, pomelo or blood orange, segmented

ORANGE CURRANT DRESSING

½ cup fresh orange juice
⅓ cup extra virgin olive oil
1 tablespoon Dijon mustard
1 teaspoon grated orange rind
2 tablespoons currants
½ teaspoon salt

Cook orzo in a pot of salted boiling water for 10 minutes until al dente and drain. Reserve some coriander leaves for garnish and finely chop the rest, stems included.

Coat chicken in paprika, thyme and ½ teaspoon salt. Heat 1 tablespoon oil in a pot and cook chicken covered until browned on both sides and cooked through. Remove and slice before serving.

Heat 2 tablespoons oil and sauté spring onions, broccolini and chopped coriander until just tender. Toss in orzo, dressing and half the almonds. Place orzo on a platter and serve topped with grapefruit, sliced smoked chicken, remaining almonds and coriander leaves.

For the **Orange Currant Dressing**, shake all ingredients together in a jar.

VARIATION For a Broccolini and Feta Orzo Salad, omit chicken and add 200g crumbled feta, mixing half through the salad and adding the rest on top.

TIPS
Store-bought smoked chicken breast or chopped barbecue chicken can be used instead of cooking your own chicken.

STYLING
Add the warm sliced chicken to the top of the salad just before serving, and sprinkle with paprika and coriander leaves.

DRINK MATCH
Chardonnay, amber ale or hefeweizen.

Main
Ratatouille Lamb

Serves 4 • Preparation time 15 minutes • Cooking time 5 ½ hours slow cooking

Combining spring lamb with new season vegetables just seems to make sense at this time of year, and my favourite way is to slow roast it to fall-apart tenderness with a French ratatouille-inspired blend of eggplant, capsicum and tomatoes. The resulting pan juices are so delectable, you will want some crusty bread to serve with it.

1 large eggplant, diced
sea salt and pepper, to taste
1 red onion, diced
4 cloves garlic, crushed
1 red capsicum, chopped
2 ripe tomatoes, diced
1 tablespoon ground cumin
1 tablespoon ground coriander
1 tablespoon smoked paprika
1kg boneless leg of lamb roast
extra virgin olive oil, for drizzling
1 bunch continental parsley leaves

Place eggplant in a large roasting tray, sprinkle with salt and stand 10 minutes. Mix in onion, garlic, capsicum, tomatoes and half the spices.

Coat lamb in remaining spices, place in the centre of the vegetables and season. Drizzle lamb and vegetables with olive oil. Wrap tray completely in two layers of foil. Slow roast at 140°C for 5 hours. Remove lamb and allow to rest, wrapped in foil.

Simmer the vegetables in the pan until reduced slightly. Season and stir in half the parsley leaves. Spoon the ratatouille onto a platter and serve topped with the lamb. Sprinkle with remaining parsley.

VARIATION Use chicken marylands in place of lamb, and only cook for 3 hours.

TIPS
Boneless leg of lamb roast is available in most supermarkets, or ask your butcher to tunnel bone it for you, rather than butterfly it.

STYLING
A deep-rimmed platter is essential to hold in those pan juices. Garnish with little parsley leaves and freshly ground pepper before serving.

DRINK MATCH
Shiraz or hazy IPA.

Starter/Main

Southern Fried Chicken Fingers with Remoulade

Serves 4 • Preparation time 20 minutes (plus 1 hour refrigeration) • Cooking time 15 minutes

Southern fried stuff takes me back to my time in New Orleans where it is more than a meal – it's a cultural icon. Here is my not-so-secret spiced flour blend that leans on the convenience of a packet of French onion soup mix to flavour the crispy coating. Serve with corn wheels and a piquant remoulade mayonnaise on the side that is perfect for dipping.

2 large chicken fillets*, skin on
1 cup buttermilk
1½ cups plain flour
35g packet French onion soup mix
3 teaspoons smoked paprika
3 teaspoons dried thyme
3 teaspoons sugar
1 teaspoon salt
1 egg
extra light olive oil or canola oil, for deep-frying
2 corn on the cob, peeled
butter, for spreading

REMOULADE
2 cornichons
1 cup mayonnaise
½ cup sour cream
1 tablespoon Dijon mustard
1 tablespoon baby capers
1 teaspoon honey
1 teaspoon paprika
tabasco or cayenne, to taste

Detach chicken tenderloin from fillet and cut the fillet into strips of the same thickness. Immerse in buttermilk and stand for at least 1 hour at room temperature or overnight in the fridge.

Combine flour with soup mix, paprika, thyme, sugar and salt. Remove chicken from milk, tossing into seasoned flour. Whisk egg into milk with a fork. After coating in flour, dip chicken in milk mixture and then double coat in flour, pressing with fingers. Allow to set on a wire rack for 10-30 minutes.

Heat oil in a wok or deep pot and deep fry chicken on medium heat until golden, crisp and cooked through*. Drain on absorbent paper and serve with Remoulade, sweetcorn wheels and extra lemon.

For the **Remoulade**, finely chop cornichons and combine with remaining ingredients.

For the **Sweetcorn Wheels**, boil, steam or microwave peeled cobs of corn until tender. Butter then cut into thin slices.

---

*If using larger chicken pieces (thighs, drumsticks, breast on the bone), they will take much longer to cook, so it's best to fry the coating and then transfer onto an oven tray with a wire rack and bake at 180°C for 15-20 minutes to cook through.

TIPS
Buttermilk can be substituted with ½ cup milk combined with ½ cup natural yoghurt or 1 cup milk plus 1 tablespoon lemon juice.

STYLING
Serve piping hot with sweetcorn wheels, cornichons, lemon wedges and a sprinkle of paprika.

DRINK MATCH
Chardonnay, riesling or German pilsner.

Side/Salad
Green Vegetable Salad with Dill Dijonnaise

Serves 4-6 • **Preparation time** 15 minutes
Cooking time 15 minutes

This salad came together the first day that Josh photographed my food. Knowing he loved his veggies, a concert of green vegetables with a creamy mustard dressing evolved.

1 large zucchini, cut lengthwise into thin slices
1 bunch young asparagus, trimmed
100g wild rocket
¼ cup frozen green peas, thawed
1 small avocado, halved
fresh dill sprigs, for garnish
sea salt and pepper, to taste

DILL DIJONNAISE
¼ cup mayonnaise
¼ cup extra virgin olive oil
1 tablespoon Dijon mustard
1 tablespoon lime or lemon juice
1 tablespoon chopped fresh dill

Poach zucchini in a frypan with ½ cup water, until just tender. Drain and cool. Cook asparagus the same way, drain, and refresh under cold water.

Layer rocket, zucchini, asparagus and peas on a platter. Position avocado halves on top. Drizzle with Dill Dijonnaise and garnish with dill, season to taste.

To make **Dill Dijonnaise**, shake all ingredients together in a screwtop jar.

Side/Salad
Baby Cucumber Salad with Olives, Pine Nuts and Tomato Dressing

Serves 4 • **Preparation time** 10 minutes

This salad is a riff on the ingredients of a Greek salad, but without the feta. Baby cucumbers are so cute and crunchy and the tomato dressing is inspired by the juice I love to mop up at the bottom of the salad bowl. Kalamata olives are perfect, and if you want to add a little feta, well that would be wonderful too.

1 large ripe heirloom tomato, finely diced
1 clove garlic, crushed
¼ cup extra virgin olive oil
sea salt, to taste
1 punnet baby cucumbers
1 tablespoon toasted pine nuts
¼ cup black kalamata olives
dried oregano, for sprinkling
fresh oregano leaves, for garnish

Combine diced tomato, garlic and oil together, season and allow to stand for 10 minutes. Cut baby cucumbers in half lengthwise and arrange on a platter.

Drizzle with tomato dressing, top with pine nuts and olives and sprinkle with dried oregano. Serve garnished with fresh oregano.

TIPS
For cucumber salad, you can use Lebanese cucumbers cut into batons. Dill Dijonnaise will keep refrigerated for two weeks.

STYLING
Always dress salads just before serving.

DRINK MATCH
For cucumber salad, rosé or fruited sour ale.
For green vegetable salad, sauvignon blanc or crisp lager.

SPRING FLINGS

Summer *love*

Summer sings of sunshine,
seafood and salads.

Summer loves stretch on the
sand and picnic in the shade.

The barbecue beckons for relaxed
entertaining as the days linger,
making the living easy.

SUMMER LOVE 63

Starter
Roast Tomato and Whipped Feta Bruschetta

Serves 6 • **Preparation time** 15 minutes • **Cooking time** 40 minutes

Broos-ket-ta is how you say it, not Broosh-etta... that's all you need to remember here. Oh, and choose sweet cherry tomatoes for the best flavour.

2 punnets cherry tomatoes, on the vine
extra virgin olive oil, as needed
sea salt and pepper, to taste
12 slices ciabatta or crusty bread
1-2 cloves garlic, peeled
2 tablespoons toasted pine nuts
fresh basil leaves, for garnish

WHIPPED FETA
200g feta cheese
¾ cup cream

Place cherry tomatoes on an oven tray, drizzle with oil, sprinkle with salt and slow roast at 150°C for 30-40 minutes until shrivelled.

Brush bread slices with oil and chargrill or grill on both sides until toasted. Rub the surface of the toasted bread with the garlic cloves.

Spread with Whipped Feta, top with cherry tomatoes and pine nuts. Drizzle with olive oil and sprinkle with basil leaves and pepper.

To make the **Whipped Feta,** blend feta and cream together in a small blender until whipped. The texture will be slightly grainy. Refrigerate to firm up until required.

VARIATION Use roasted capsicum instead of the slow-roasted tomatoes or use cream cheese or ricotta in place of feta.

TIPS
Slow-roasted tomatoes will keep refrigerated for 2 days. Whipped feta can be made up to 1 week in advance.

STYLING
Flutter basil leaves from a height to garnish the dish.

DRINK MATCH
Sparkling rosé or Italian pilsner.

SUMMER LOVE

Starter
King Prawn Pâté with Tortilla Crisps

Serves 4-6 • **Preparation time** 20 minutes • **Cooking time** 10 minutes

This is an elegant answer to boring old dip - deliciously decadent prawns and mascarpone served with crisp tortilla chips. When I want to glam it up a little more for cocktail parties, I serve the prawn pâté with lavosh crackers and salmon caviar.

250g cooked king prawns, peeled
2 spring onions, finely chopped
1 tablespoon chopped dill
1 tablespoon lemon juice
125g mascarpone or sour cream
½ teaspoon sriracha or tabasco hot sauce
sea salt, to taste
4 round flour tortillas
olive oil spray

Chop the prawns and combine with spring onions, dill, lemon juice, mascarpone and sriracha, and season to taste. Refrigerate until slightly firm.

Spray tortillas on both sides with olive oil and cut into long wedges. Bake at 200°C for 5-10 minutes until golden brown.

Serve pâté with Tortilla Crisps.

VARIATION Prawn Pâté Picnic Breadstick: Hollow out the centre of a small breadstick from the ends, leaving it mostly intact. Fill with prawn pâté, wrap and refrigerate until firm. Serve cut into slices.

TIPS
Tortilla crisps will keep for a week in an airtight container.

STYLING
Garnish with one prawn, a drizzle of chilli sauce and a few dill sprigs.

DRINK MATCH
Sauvignon blanc, crisp lager or fruited sour ale.

Starter

Zucchini Dill Fritters with Brie and Plum Chutney

Making small fritters means you can top them and serve them as pop-in-the-mouth savouries. A wedge of brie and a dollop of chutney turns them into pretty pass-arounds, but you can also top them with goat's cheese and an olive or smoked salmon and make an assortment for a platter.

Zucchini Dill Fritters

Makes 16 • **Preparation time** 15 minutes
Cooking time 10 minutes

250g brie or camembert
200g zucchini, grated
1 tablespoon chopped fresh dill
¼ cup self-raising flour
2 eggs
sea salt and pepper, to taste
extra light olive oil or canola oil, for shallow frying
Plum Chutney, for dolloping
dill sprigs, for garnish

Bring brie to room temperature. Combine zucchini, dill, flour and eggs together and season. Heat oil in a large frypan and shallow fry tablespoons of mixture for 1-2 minutes on each side until golden brown, to make 16 fritters. Cut brie into 16 wedges. Place a wedge of brie on each hot fritter. Dollop with chutney, garnish with dill and serve hot.

Homemade Plum Chutney

Makes 4 cups

1kg fresh blood plums, halved and stoned
2 red apples, cored and diced
4 red onions, diced
2 cups red wine vinegar
1 cup dark brown sugar
1 cup sultanas or raisins
1 tablespoon sea salt
1 teaspoon chilli flakes
2 cinnamon sticks
a few sprigs fresh thyme

Combine all ingredients in a large pot and bring to the boil, stirring until the sugar dissolves. Reduce to a simmer and simmer uncovered, stirring occasionally, until thick. Spoon into sterilised jars, seal and store in the fridge.

TIPS
Fritters can be made ahead of time and warmed in the oven for a few minutes before serving.

STYLING
Use a tiny pointed spoon and drop the chutney vertically onto the food to achieve that perfect dollop.

DRINK MATCH
Sparkling or farmhouse ale.

Salad/Side

Spanish Orange and Fennel Salad

Serves 4-6 • **Preparation time** 15 minutes

The success of this salad relies on some very fine knife skills to pare the orange skin before thinly slicing the orange, to shave the fennel and finely slice the onion, so that each element combines in a mouthful of freshness and zest.

3 oranges
1 small red onion, thinly sliced into rings
1 teaspoon salt
1 bulb fennel, fronds retained
extra virgin olive oil, as needed
½ cup black olives
sea salt and pepper, to taste

Juice one orange. Using a paring knife, cut the skin and pith from the remaining oranges and slice thinly. Combine onion, orange juice and salt and allow to stand for 10 minutes.

Reserve the fennel fronds for garnish. Remove the tough stalks and finely slice the bulb. Drizzle fennel with oil and season.

Layer fennel, oranges, onion rings and olives onto a serving platter.

Drizzle with orange juice and olive oil. Season with pepper and garnish with fennel fronds.

VARIATION Use blood oranges when in season; green olives can be used in place of black.

TIPS
Use a mandolin to shave the fennel and onion as finely as possible.

STYLING
Take care to remove all the skin and pith from the oranges before slicing.

DRINK MATCH
Sauvignon blanc, pinot grigio, saison or Australian pale ale.

Side/Snack

Charred Corn with Maple Butter

Serves 4 • **Preparation time** 10 minutes • **Cooking time** 20 minutes

When I was ten, we travelled to Greece and it was the first time I had corn grilled over the coals, from a street vendor in Athens. I remember that first taste of sweet, chewy, charcoaled sweetcorn and the delight of holding it like a lollipop and nibbling away as we roamed the streets. I remember my sister and I begging Mum for another one whenever we passed the vendors. In later years, I would challenge my kids to a corn race to get them to quickly eat up every niblet and still now, charred corn slathered in a flavoured butter is a barbecue favourite.

125g butter, softened
2 tablespoons maple syrup
4 corn on the cob with husks
sea salt, for sprinkling
chilli flakes, for sprinkling

Blend butter with maple syrup until smooth.

Peel back the husks on the corn, removing the silk. Remove the coarse outer leaves, and tie the remainder together using a strip of leaf.

Chargrill on all sides until lightly blackened. Butter all over and sprinkle with salt and chilli to taste.

Serve with a knob of Maple Butter on top.

VARIATION Chilli flakes can be swapped with smoked paprika, chopped herbs or a good sprinkle of grated parmesan. Honey or sweet chilli sauce can be used in place of maple syrup.

TIPS
Fresh corn will lose sweetness the longer it is stored, so use it soon after buying.

STYLING
Always sprinkle spice or herbs from a height and the dish almost designs itself!

DRINK MATCH
Pinot grigio or hazy pale ale.

Starter

Grilled Sardines with Green Olive Salsa and Garlic Croutons

Serves 4-8 • **Preparation time** 15 minutes • **Cooking time** 15 minutes

Sardines done this way always remind me of visiting my aunt in Thessaloniki, who spent the afternoon carefully deboning them before quickly charring them over an open fire in the heat of a Greek summer. The olive salsa adds a piquant touch to the deep flavour of the sardines.

500g fresh sardines, cleaned
extra virgin olive oil
sea salt, to taste
¼ cup fresh oregano leaves
lime or lemon wedges, for serving

GREEN OLIVE SALSA
¼ cup pitted grilled green olives*, sliced
1 clove garlic, crushed
1 spring onion, chopped
2 tablespoons chopped continental parsley
½-1 teaspoon chopped chilli, to taste
1 tablespoon balsamic vinegar
¼ cup extra virgin olive oil

GARLIC CROUTONS
2 slices mixed grain bread, cut into cubes
olive oil, for drizzling
1 teaspoon garlic salt
1 teaspoon paprika
1 teaspoon dried thyme
½ teaspoon salt

Lightly coat sardines with oil and season with salt. Cook on a hot barbecue and chargrill, or grill for a few minutes on each side, until just cooked.

Transfer to a platter, top with Green Olive Salsa, crumbled Garlic Croutons and oregano leaves.

Serve with lime wedges.

For the **Green Olive Salsa,** combine all ingredients together and use as required.

For the **Garlic Croutons,** place bread cubes on an oven tray, drizzle with oil and toss with remaining ingredients. Bake at 200°C for 5-10 minutes until golden brown.

*****VARIATION** If grilled olives are not available, use regular or stuffed green olives.

TIPS
Try the Green Olive Salsa over a piece of pan-fried fish fillet.

STYLING
Arrange sardines side by side and spoon salsa across the middle of the sardines, then layer with croutons and herbs.

DRINK MATCH
Rosé, saison or fruited sour ale.

Starter
Red Wine Octopus with Feta Dressing

Serves 6 • Preparation time 10 minutes (plus refrigeration time) • Cooking time 30 minutes

Pickled octopus always reminds me of sitting in a seaside Greek taverna, nibbling on mezze between lazy beach swims. Baby octopus with a zesty feta dressing evokes the same feeling for me.

2 cups water
1 onion, quartered
2 cloves garlic, peeled
1 teaspoon peppercorns
1kg cleaned baby octopus
1 cup dry red wine
100g feta cheese, crumbled
1 tablespoon fresh oregano, finely chopped
1 clove garlic, crushed
¼ cup extra virgin olive oil
juice of 1 lemon
extra oregano, for garnish
freshly ground black pepper

Combine water, onion, garlic cloves and peppercorns in a pot and bring to the boil. Add octopus and wine and simmer covered for 30 minutes, until tender. Allow to cool and refrigerate until chilled (overnight if required).

Combine feta, oregano, crushed garlic, oil and lemon juice together to make a dressing. Serve drained octopus topped with dressing, extra oregano and a sprinkling of pepper.

Starter
Summertime Fennel Mussels

Serves 4 • Preparation time 20 minutes
Cooking time 15 minutes

Summer holiday food doesn't get better than sourcing local mussels and cooking them simply, Provençale style, in a pot of aromatics that is just begging to be mopped up with crusty bread.

¼ cup extra virgin olive oil
1 bulb fennel, finely diced; retain fronds for garnish
1 red capsicum, finely diced
3 cloves garlic, crushed
2kg mussels, scrubbed and debearded
4 ripe tomatoes, diced
1 cup pinot grigio wine
60g butter

Heat the oil in a large pot and sauté the fennel, capsicum and garlic until softened.

Add mussels, tomatoes and wine and simmer covered until mussels open (approximately 10 minutes).

Stir in butter and serve garnished with fennel fronds.

VARIATION Use celery in place of fennel.

TIPS
If using frozen octopus, thaw overnight in the fridge.
For mussels, serve with homemade potato chips and garlic aioli.

STYLING
For octopus, keep a little crumbled feta to sprinkle on top when serving.
For mussels, keep fennel fronds in iced water to freshen them up before using to garnish.

DRINK MATCH
For octopus, serve with pinot noir or session IPA.
For mussels, serve with sauvignon blanc or Australian pale ale.

Salad
Egyptian Fattoush Salad

Serves 8 • **Preparation time** 15 minutes • **Cooking time** 15 minutes

I vividly remember my first taste of this salad in Cairo, just before we headed out to see the after-dark sound and light show at The Sphinx. It was delivered to our table on a giant tray, balanced high on the waiter's shoulder, that was laden with an assortment of Middle Eastern mezze. It combines freshness and crunch in the most textural way, and the last minute tossing together is essential to keep the vegetables vibrant and the pita crisps as crunchy as possible.

1 large pita bread
extra virgin olive oil
sea salt, to taste
allspice, to taste
1 Lebanese cucumber
1 small cos lettuce, shredded
4 large tomatoes, diced
4 radishes, finely sliced
2 spring onions, chopped
1 small red capsicum, cut into strips
½ bunch continental parsley leaves
½ bunch mint leaves
juice of 1 lemon
sumac or dukkah, for sprinkling

Split the pita bread into 2 rounds. Brush with olive oil, place on an oven tray and season with salt and allspice. Bake at 200°C for 10-15 minutes until golden brown and crisp.

Cut cucumber in half lengthwise. Scoop out seeds and cut into slices.

Layer lettuce, cucumber, tomatoes, radishes, spring onions, capsicum, parsley and mint leaves onto a large platter.

Shake lemon juice and ½ cup olive oil together in a jar and dress salad, seasoning with salt and tossing lightly.

Break toasted pita into pieces and stir in just before serving.

Serve sprinkled liberally with sumac or dukkah.

VARIATION Add chargrilled prawns for an exotic main course salad.

TIPS
Crunchy pita crisps are a great way to use leftover pita bread, and they store well in a jar.

STYLING
Use a salad spinner to wash and dry both lettuce and herbs to ensure the salad looks fresh and bouncy.

DRINK MATCH
Sauvignon blanc, crisp lager or saison.

82

TASTE*ful*

Main/Starter

Chargrilled Quail with Freekeh and Pomegranate Salad

Serves 6 as a main, 12 as a starter • **Preparation time** 15 minutes (plus 1 hour marinating) • **Cooking time** 15 minutes

This ancient grain salad has become a firm family favourite and when you partner it with delicate chargrilled quail it suddenly becomes a banquet.

1 bunch fresh mint
6 partially deboned jumbo quail*
4 cloves garlic, crushed
sea salt and pepper, to taste
1 teaspoon chilli flakes
extra virgin olive oil, as needed
2 tablespoons pomegranate molasses
2 tablespoons honey
⅓ cup currants
juice of 1 large lemon
1 cup whole or cracked freekeh
400g can lentils, rinsed and drained
3 spring onions, chopped
½ cup chopped continental parsley
1 pomegranate, seeds and juice
¼ cup toasted slivered almonds

For the quail, finely chop mint stalks and leaves separately, retaining some leaves for garnish. Combine mint stalks with quail, garlic, 1 teaspoon salt, chilli and 2 tablespoons oil. Marinate for 1 hour at room temperature or refrigerate overnight.

For the salad dressing, shake pomegranate molasses, 1 tablespoon honey and 2 tablespoons oil together in a jar. Combine currants, 1 tablespoon honey and lemon juice in a small bowl.

Place freekeh, 1 litre water and 1 tablespoon salt in a saucepan and boil for 15 minutes until tender. Drain, rinsing briefly, and cool. Toss freekeh together with lentils, currant mixture, spring onions, parsley, chopped mint, pomegranate juice, half the pomegranate seeds, half the almonds and ½ cup oil, and season to taste.

To serve, chargrill quail for 5 minutes on each side, until golden and done to your liking (quail is best served a little pink). Portion salad onto plates, top with quail, dressing, remaining pomegranate, almonds and mint leaves.

VARIATION Roasted baby beetroot can be added to the salad or used in place of the quail for a vegan option.

TIPS
*Partially deboned quail is sometimes sold as butterflied quail. The recipe can be made with boned quail too, it just means it is a little more fiddly to eat!

STYLING
Use a large platter to show off the food.

DRINK MATCH
Sangiovese or red ale.

SUMMER LOVE

Main

Prawn, Pea and Pistachio Linguine

Serves 6 • **Preparation time** 10 minutes • **Cooking time** 20 minutes

This elegant pasta dish is so speedy to put together that it turns a midweek meal at home into an Italian bistro experience. It is restaurant quality and comfort food all at the same time, and when it comes to pasta, well, you know I love to twirl!

500g linguine pasta
750g frozen green prawn cutlets, semi-thawed
50g butter
2 cloves garlic, crushed
2 cups pinot grigio
2 cups cream
sea salt, to taste
1 cup frozen peas
2 spring onions, chopped
½ bunch basil leaves
¼ cup chopped pistachio nuts

Cook the pasta in a pot of salted boiling water until al dente.

Meanwhile, split each semi-thawed prawn in half lengthways using a sharp knife, keeping the tail on one half.

Drain the pasta, reserving 1 cup of pasta water.

Melt butter in the pot and sauté garlic until softened. Add pinot grigio and cream and bring to the boil. Simmer for 5 minutes until slightly reduced. Season with salt.

Add prawns, peas and spring onions to the pot, and simmer until prawns are just cooked.

Stir in pasta and basil leaves, retaining some for garnish. Add a little pasta water if needed.

Serve in pasta bowls, sprinkled with pistachio nuts and pepper and garnished with basil leaves.

VARIATION Use scallops with roe in place of prawns.

TIPS
Any long pasta - linguine, spaghetti, fettucine or tagliatelle - can be used in this recipe.

STYLING
Turn the serving plate while you position the linguine in the centre of it using tongs, to achieve a swirled pasta effect.

DRINK MATCH
Pinot grigio or German pilsner.

SUMMER LOVE 85

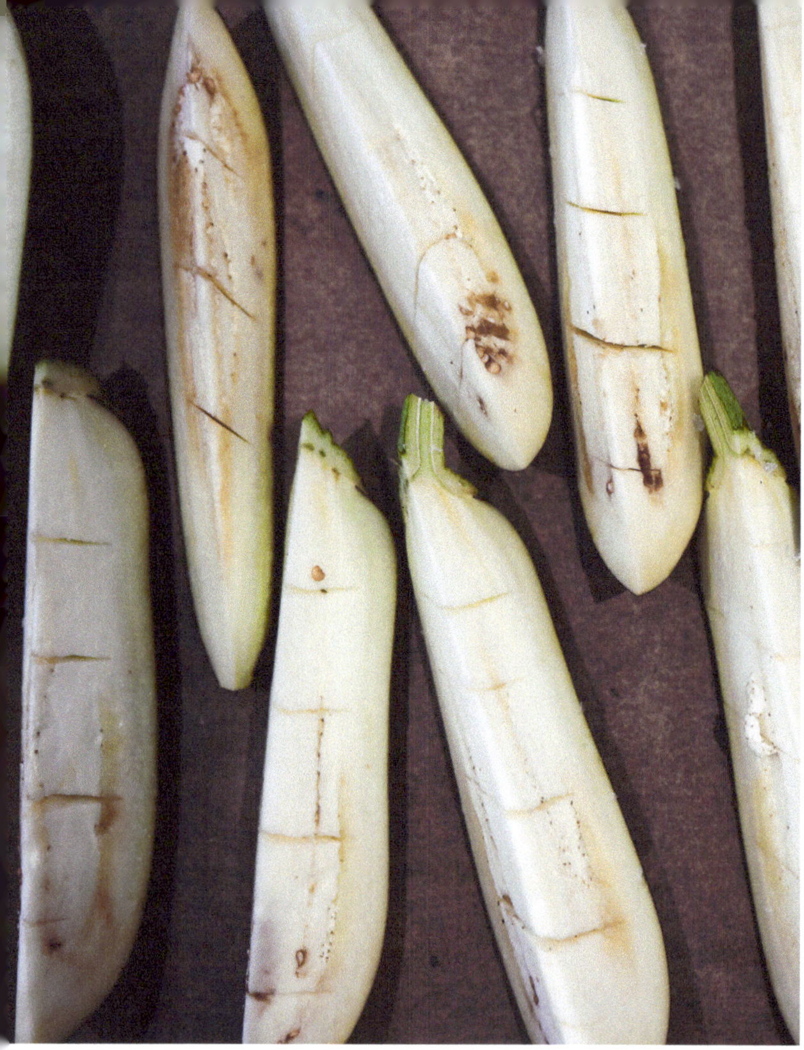

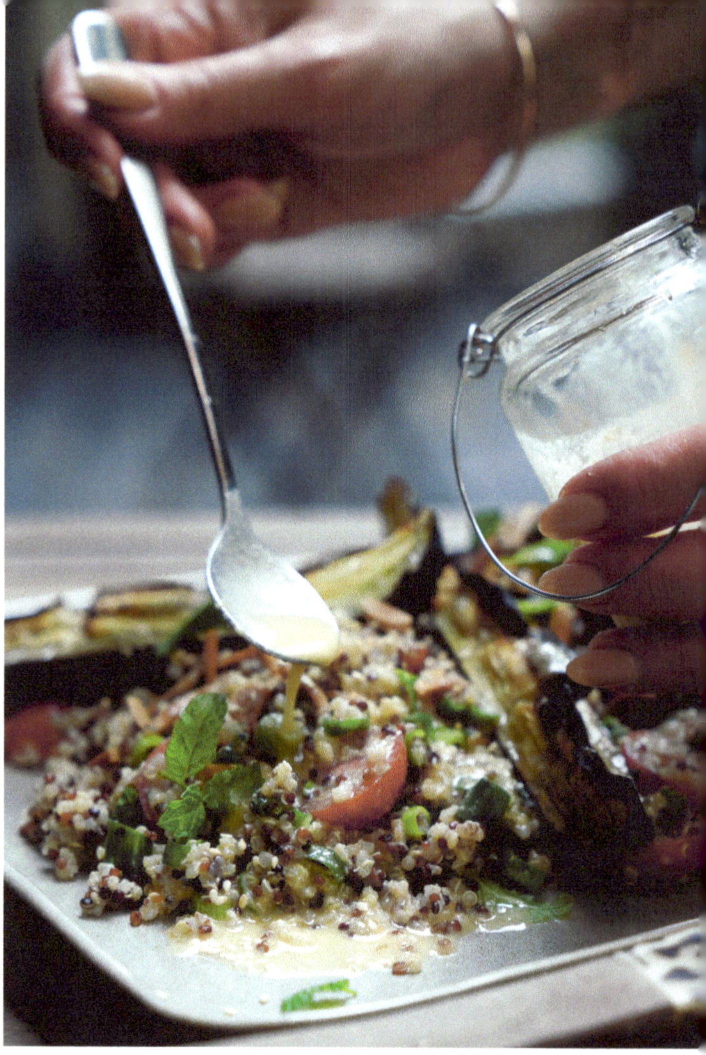

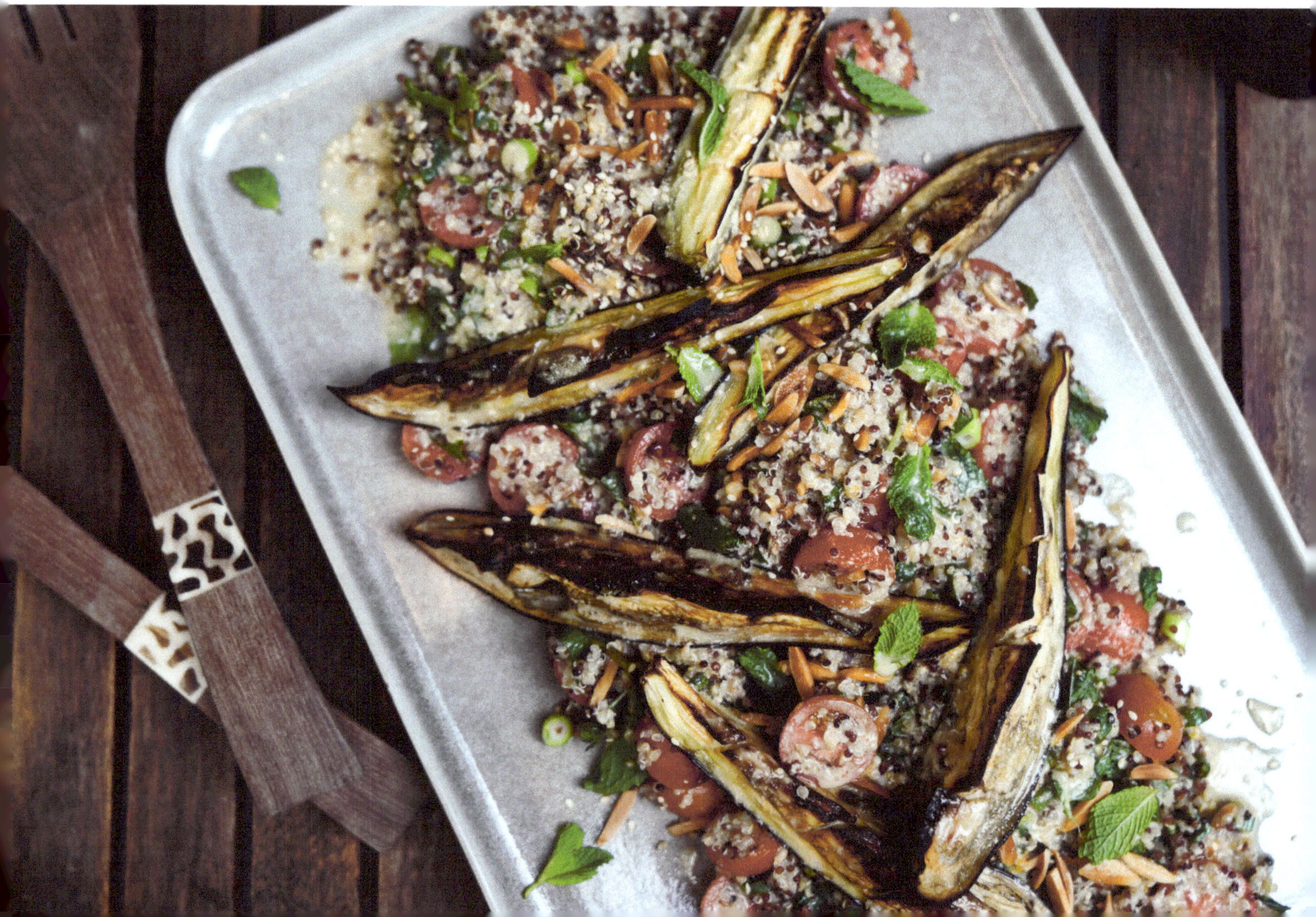

Main/Salad

Sesame Eggplant Quinoa with Orange Tahini Dressing

Serves 4-6 • **Preparation time** 15 minutes • **Cooking time** 30 minutes

This is a sensational side but it is also a wonderful meatless meal. Roasted eggplant wedges become the highlight of the dish, making it very satisfying. I grew up watching my dad vigorously mixing the tahini to serve with meats and falafel. That very-adult, nutty but slightly bitter taste took some getting used to, decades in fact, but now I love mixing it with sweet citrus to balance its savouriness.

1 cup quinoa
1 large eggplant
sea salt and pepper, to taste
extra virgin olive oil, as needed
1 punnet cherry tomatoes, halved
2 spring onions, chopped
1 cup torn mint leaves
¼ cup toasted slivered almonds
1 tablespoon toasted sesame seeds

ORANGE TAHINI DRESSING
2 tablespoons tahini
½ cup fresh orange juice
¼ cup extra virgin olive oil
½ teaspoon salt

Soak quinoa in 2 cups water in a pot for 15 minutes.

Cut eggplant into 4 or 6 long wedges, and make slashes in the flesh. Season liberally with salt and allow to stand for 15 minutes. Wipe salt off eggplant with absorbent paper then place on an oven tray. Drizzle with oil and roast at 200°C in the upper half of the oven for 30 minutes until golden brown.

Add 1 teaspoon salt to quinoa, bring to the boil and simmer covered for 15 minutes. Then turn off the stove and allow to stand for 10 minutes. Mix 2 tablespoons olive oil into quinoa and season.

Toss in tomatoes, spring onions, mint, almonds and half of the Orange Tahini Dressing. Arrange on a platter. Place roasted eggplant wedges on top. Drizzle with remaining dressing and sprinkle with sesame seeds.

For the **Orange Tahini Dressing**, shake all ingredients together, blending with a fork if needed. Use as required.

TIPS
Quinoa (keen-wa) is an ancient crop dating back to the Incas. It is technically a seed, not a grain, and is a great alternative to wheat and rice. It comes in white, red and black varieties. I used tricolour in this recipe.

STYLING
Arrange quinoa on a large platter, top with eggplant wedges and drizzle dressing in a zig zag pattern with a small spoon to let the eggplant shine through. Sprinkle with seeds just before serving.

DRINK MATCH
Riesling, pinot gris or fruited sour ale.

Main/Salad

Za'atar and Haloumi Lamb Cutlets with Esme Salad

Makes 12 • **Preparation time** 10 minutes • **Cooking time** 10 minutes

Oh how I love lamb cutlets - tender sweet little morsels of meat with a convenient built-in handle. It's fun to tuck in a little haloumi to form a surprise centre, and coat them in spice before they hit the barbecue. Here I've served them with a crunchy and colourful Turkish Esme Salad that is a great contrast to any barbecued meats.

12 large lamb cutlets, trimmed
120g haloumi cheese, drained
za'atar* or dukkah spices, for sprinkling
lemon wedges, for serving
extra virgin olive oil, for drizzling

ESME SALAD

1 punnet cherry tomatoes, cut into wedges
1 red onion, finely diced
2 cloves garlic, crushed
1 large green capsicum, finely diced
1 large red capsicum, finely diced
1 cup chopped continental parsley
2 tablespoons tomato paste
2 tablespoons pomegranate molasses or balsamic glaze
1 teaspoon chilli flakes
½ cup extra virgin olive oil
2 teaspoons salt

Using a sharp pointed knife, cut a deep pocket into the side of each lamb cutlet. Cut haloumi into 12 squares. Insert a square of haloumi into each cutlet, reshaping it to enclose the cheese.

Season cutlets on both sides with za'atar spices. Barbecue cutlets for 3-4 minutes on each side until they are browned and haloumi has softened.

Serve hot on a bed of Esme Salad with a squeeze of lemon juice and drizzle of oil.

For the **Esme Salad**, combine all the ingredients together and serve with cutlets. The salad may be made up to 1 day before.

---

*Za'atar Spice Blend: *Combine 1 tablespoon each of sesame seeds, dried thyme, ground cumin, dried oregano, sumac and sea salt.*

TIPS
Make up a jar of za'atar to keep in your pantry to sprinkle a little Middle Eastern flavour into dishes.

STYLING
Perch the cutlets on mounds of salad with the cutlet bones upward, so they are easy to grab.

DRINK MATCH
Montepulciano or Australian pale ale.

SUMMER LOVE

Main

Spice-rubbed Duck Legs with Roast Nectarines and Cherries

Serves 4 • **Preparation time** 30 minutes (plus 1 hour standing time) • **Cooking time** 2 ½ hours

The richness of duck meat loves the zing of summer fruits and when you add a touch of spice, the result is three-dimensional, taste-wise. Once you rub in the spices, the oven will slow roast it to tenderness for you and the roasted nectarines and cherries will soften to form a bright compote to serve the duck on. This dish is quite fancy in looks, but totally easy to do.

4 duck legs, trimmed
extra virgin olive oil, for drizzling

SPICE RUB
1 tablespoon fine salt
1 tablespoon ground cumin
2 teaspoons garlic salt
2 teaspoons paprika
1 teaspoon cinnamon
1 teaspoon freshly ground
  black pepper

**ROASTED NECTARINES
AND CHERRIES**
250g nectarines, cut into wedges
125g cherries, on stem
2 teaspoons dark brown sugar
½ teaspoon salt
2 teaspoons fresh thyme leaves
freshly ground black pepper

Combine all the ingredients for the **Spice Rub** together. Coat the duck legs all over with the spice rub; allow to stand at room temperature for 1 hour, or refrigerate overnight and bring to room temperature before cooking.

Place in a roasting dish and drizzle with olive oil. Roast at 200°C for 30 minutes. Cover with foil, reduce the temperature to 150°C and slow roast for 1 ½ hours until very tender.

Serve on a bed of Roasted Nectarines and Cherries garnished with thyme.

For the **Roasted Nectarines and Cherries**, arrange nectarines and cherries on a baking paper-lined oven tray and sprinkle with sugar, salt and thyme. Season with pepper. Roast at 220°C for 20 minutes. May be served warm or allowed to cool before serving.

VARIATION Use dark grapes and canned plums when stonefruit is not in season.

TIPS
Chicken marylands can be used instead of the duck.

STYLING
Arrange the roasted fruit on the centre of the plate and rest the duck on top, with the leg pointing upwards. Finish the dish with a drizzle of oil, a sprinkle of spice and some fresh thyme sprigs.

DRINK MATCH
Pinot noir or cloudy apple cider.

Main

Sumac Chicken with Apple Mint Salad and Cranberries

Serves 4 as a main course • **Preparation time** 30 minutes • **Cooking time** 15 minutes

This is so much more than a chicken salad, particularly if you cook and carve the chicken and serve the warm slices on top of the fresh salad mix. Add an extra shake of sumac for a little more tang.

750g chicken fillets (skin on)
sea salt, as required
sumac, for sprinkling
juice of 2 limes
⅓ cup extra light olive oil
2 tablespoons honey
⅓ cup dried cranberries (craisins)
1 large green apple, cut into matchstick strips
1 baby cos lettuce, shredded
80g baby rocket leaves
1 cup chopped mint leaves
1 Lebanese cucumber, cut in half lengthwise, deseeded and sliced
2 spring onions, chopped
2 tablespoons toasted slivered almonds
mint leaves, for garnish

Season chicken with 1 tablespoon salt and 1 tablespoon sumac and allow to come to room temperature.

Meanwhile, combine lime juice, oil, honey, 1 teaspoon salt, cranberries and apple together and allow to stand.

Chargrill chicken for 5-10 minutes on each side until cooked through and rest for 5 minutes (if chicken fillets are very large, roast in oven for 10 minutes to complete cooking).

Toss lettuce, rocket, mint, cucumber, spring onions and half the almonds together with the apple mixture.

Slice the chicken and layer chicken and salad into a serving bowl.

Serve garnished with remaining almonds, extra mint leaves and a sprinkling of sumac.

VARIATION The salad is a great accompaniment for a store-bought roast chicken.

TIPS
To get honey out of the jar easily, heat a metal spoon over a flame before using it and the honey will just slip off.

STYLING
Layer instead of tossing salads for a more composed look.

DRINK MATCH
Chardonnay or cloudy apple cider.

Main

Italian Veal with Tuna and Caper Sauce and Asparagus

Serves 6 • **Preparation time** 30 minutes • **Cooking time** 1 ½ hours

This is my take on vitello tonnato which is the perfect alfresco summer dish. I like to add elegant asparagus spears to finish the platter. The girello can be cooked and the mayonnaise made the day before for easy serving later.

900g-1kg piece veal girello (nut of veal)
sea salt and pepper, to taste
1 tablespoon extra virgin olive oil
1 onion, quartered
3 stalks celery, chopped
2 carrots, chopped
2 cloves garlic, peeled
2 cups dry white wine
1 litre water
½ lemon, sliced
continental parsley, capers and cornichons, for garnish
2 bunches asparagus, steamed, for serving

TUNA AND CAPER SAUCE
185g can tuna in oil, undrained
1 tablespoon capers
4 anchovies
2 egg yolks
¼ cup extra virgin olive oil
1 tablespoon lemon juice

Season veal. Heat oil in a large pot. Brown veal on all sides and remove. Add vegetables, wine, water, lemon and a few sprigs of parsley to the pot and bring to the boil. Return veal to pot, cover and turn off the heat. Allow to stand without disturbing for 1 ½ hours until it cools, at which time the meat should be poached but still pink. Note that some of the cooking liquid may be used in the making of the Tuna and Caper Sauce. The veal may be refrigerated at this stage if being made in advance.

To serve, thinly slice the veal. Spread serving plates with Tuna and Caper Sauce and arrange veal slices on top. Drizzle with more sauce and garnish with extra capers, parsley, halved cornichons and freshly ground black pepper. Serve with steamed asparagus tossed in olive oil.

For the **Tuna and Caper Sauce**, combine tuna in oil, capers, anchovies and yolks in a blender and blend to a paste. Gradually add ¼ cup olive oil while blending until smooth. Blend in lemon juice. Add a little of the cooled cooking liquid from the veal to adjust to desired consistency. Use as required, keeping refrigerated if being made in advance.

TIPS
To double the recipe, use two pieces of girello and double the sauce, but there is no need to double the poaching liquid.

STYLING
Always sauce just before serving.

DRINK MATCH
Soave, pinot grigio, or German wheat beer.

Starter/Main
Stuffed Zucchini Wrapped in Prosciutto

Serves 4 • **Preparation time** 15 minutes • **Cooking time** 45 minutes

When my husband came home one afternoon carrying a little basket of homegrown zucchini and tomatoes from my dad-in-law's garden, I knew I had to put as much care into the recipe choice as he does into his abundant backyard veggie patch. Each year I am amazed at how everything grows to a lush fruitfulness under his hand. It reminds me to take the time and have the patience to nurture something to its full potential.

2 large zucchini (approx 500g each)
2 tablespoons olive oil
1 onion, finely chopped
2 cloves garlic, chopped
1 red capsicum, finely chopped
2 ripe tomatoes, finely chopped
1 teaspoon fennel seeds
sea salt and pepper, to taste
2 tablespoons toasted pine nuts
12 slices prosciutto
parsley leaves, for garnish

Cut the zucchini in half lengthwise. Use a melon baller or small spoon to hollow out the flesh of the zucchini, keeping the shell intact. Chop the flesh.

Heat oil in a pot and sauté onion, garlic, capsicum, zucchini flesh, tomatoes and fennel seeds. Cook for 5 minutes until softened and season to taste.

Spoon filling back into zucchini shells. Sprinkle with pine nuts and wrap slices of prosciutto around the zucchini, enclosing the filling.

Place on an oven tray, drizzle with olive oil and sprinkle with pepper. Bake at 200°C for 40 minutes until zucchini has softened.

Serve drizzled with olive oil and garnish with parsley.

VARIATION Eggplant can be used instead of zucchini but roast the eggplant halves for 30 minutes before scooping out the flesh to use in the recipe.

TIPS
These can be made with small zucchini and served as an entrée or side dish. They are delicious served with tzatziki on the side.

STYLING
Wrap the prosciutto around the zucchini on a slight diagonal before roasting. Garnish with small parsley leaves just prior to serving.

DRINK MATCH
Arneis or farmhouse ale.

SUMMER LOVE

Main
Slow-roasted Salmon with Salad Verde and Smoky Aioli

Serves 8 • **Preparation time** 30 minutes • **Cooking time** 30 minutes

This is my Christmas salmon extravaganza that looks so festive as a centrepiece on the table but is actually very easy to prepare. The key is to not overcook the salmon; pink is definitely preferred here.

1.5kg side of salmon, pin-boned
baking paper
2 tablespoons toasted pine nuts
seeds from ½ pomegranate

SALAD VERDE
½ cup each of torn basil, dill, parsley and mint leaves
3 spring onions, finely chopped
8 anchovy fillets, chopped
⅓ cup chopped cornichons
⅓ cup baby capers

SMOKY AIOLI
1 cup aioli or good quality egg mayonnaise
1 tablespoon smoked paprika

Place salmon on a sheet of baking paper on an oven tray and cover with a second sheet. Bake at 150°C for 20-25 minutes and allow to cool. The fish will continue to cook on standing but will be medium-rare in the thickest part.

Combine herbs, spring onions, anchovies, cornichons and capers together to make **Salad Verde**. Combine aioli and smoked paprika together to make **Smoky Aioli**.

Just before serving, spread salmon with Smoky Aioli and sprinkle with the Salad Verde, pine nuts and pomegranate seeds.

VARIATION You can also make this dish with pieces of salmon fillet for individual portions. Just reduce cooking time to 10-15 minutes until salmon is medium-rare.

TIPS
Cooked salmon can be left at room temperature for up to an hour before serving.

STYLING
Assemble the dish just prior to serving and select some tiny herb leaves to sprinkle on top.

DRINK MATCH
Chardonnay, sparkling rosé or hazy pale ale.

Main
Minted Lamb Kofta with Beetroot Cacik

Serves 6 • **Preparation time** 30 minutes • **Cooking time** 40 minutes

Middle Eastern meatballs are so full of flavour and are just as tasty chargrilled, barbecued or pan-fried. I like to serve them with Beetroot Cacik, which is the Turkish answer to Greek tzatziki and adds colour and zest to the plate.

1kg lamb mince
½ cup chopped mint
½ cup chopped continental parsley
2 spring onions, finely chopped
2 tablespoons smoked paprika
2 tablespoons ground cumin
1 tablespoon garlic salt
1 teaspoon salt
pita bread, for serving

BEETROOT CACIK
1 beetroot (250g)
1 clove garlic, crushed
2 tablespoons chopped mint
2 teaspoons sea salt
1 tablespoon extra virgin olive oil
1 cup Greek-style yoghurt

Combine all ingredients together and mix well using your hands. Form large spoonfuls of mixture into oval shapes and cook on an oiled chargrill for 10-15 minutes, turning to brown evenly. Serve with Beetroot Cacik and chargrilled pita bread.

For the **Beetroot Cacik**, roast beetroot at 200°C for 30-40 minutes until tender. Allow to cool, remove skin and grate flesh. Combine with garlic, mint, salt and oil and swirl in yoghurt, leaving it a little marbled in appearance. Refrigerate until chilled. Drizzle with olive oil and sprinkle with mint leaves.

VARIATION Beef, pork or chicken mince can be used in place of the lamb mince. Use 1 seeded and grated Lebanese cucumber instead of beetroot to make Greek tzatziki instead. Dill can be used instead of mint.

TIPS
Make double the kofta and freeze some for a quick and easy dinner another time.

STYLING
Chargrill kofta horizontally across the grill to achieve those 'zebra' stripes. Serve on skewers after cooking.

DRINK MATCH
Riesling or hazy pale ale.

Dessert/Cheese

Buffalo Mozzarella with Nectarines, Honey and Petals

Serves 4 • **Preparation time** 5 minutes

This is a whimsical dish that looks as pretty as it tastes. Serve it after a meal instead of the cheese course or dessert, or just make it because it tastes lush and looks divine.

200g buffalo mozzarella bocconcini, drained
2 fresh nectarines or peaches, cut into wedges
extra virgin olive oil, for drizzling
honey, for drizzling
sea salt and pepper, to taste
edible petals, for garnish

Tear bocconcini into pieces and arrange on a serving plate with nectarines.

Drizzle with oil and honey.

Sprinkle with salt, pepper and edible petals.

VARIATION Burrata or stracchino cheese make a great alternative to buffalo mozzarella.

TIPS
Fresh edible petals are available at gourmet greengrocers. You can use edible garden flowers like nasturtiums and rose petals, but be sure they haven't been sprayed!

STYLING
Drizzle honey boldly across the plate from a height for a thin, continuous drizzle.

DRINK MATCH
Sparkling or farmhouse ale.

SUMMER LOVE 105

A crowd pleasing grazing table

Autumn
passions

In Autumn, the earthy colours on the plate echo the crunch of the fallen leaves.

We turn inside towards our passions. To take a little longer with our flavours. To find time to share.

AUTUMN PASSIONS

Starter/Snack
Magic Mushrooms on Toast

Serves 6 • **Preparation time** 10 minutes • **Cooking time** 10 minutes

The combination of Swiss brown and porcini mushrooms with the scent of thyme, served atop toasted grainy bread, is what makes these magic. It's perfect brunch food for any time of the year.

10g dried porcini mushrooms
150g Swiss brown mushrooms, sliced
extra virgin olive oil, as needed
4 cloves garlic, crushed
2 teaspoons fresh thyme leaves
sea salt and pepper, to taste
6 slices multigrain sourdough bread
100g fresh buffalo or cow's ricotta
¼ cup toasted pine nuts

Soak porcini mushrooms in ½ cup boiling water for 10 minutes. Use scissors to finely chop porcini mushrooms, reserving liquid.

Heat 2 tablespoons oil in a frypan and sauté garlic and Swiss brown mushrooms until softened. Add porcini mushrooms, reserved liquid and thyme and cook, stirring, until liquid has mostly evaporated. Season.

Brush bread on both sides with olive oil and chargrill or grill on both sides until golden. Spread with ricotta and sprinkle with half the pine nuts. Top with warm mushroom mixture, drizzle with oil and serve sprinkled with remaining pine nuts, pepper and extra thyme.

VARIATION Add a little chopped bacon when sautéing the mushrooms.

TIPS
To make this extra special, season mushrooms with truffle salt or mix in some truffle paste.

STYLING
Whip the ricotta with a butter knife before spreading, to create creamy 'waves'.

DRINK MATCH
Chardonnay or American strong ale.

Starter/Side

Roast Capsicum with Feta and Olives

Serves 4 • **Preparation time** 10 minutes • **Cooking time** 15 minutes

This is a very Greek way to serve capsicums. The best way to eat them is to mash them together with the feta using a fork, and then slap it all on some grilled pita bread. A little Greek music in the background is recommended for the full experience.

4 red capsicums (bullhorn variety, if available)
200g feta cheese
¼ cup black kalamata olives
extra virgin olive oil, for drizzling
dried Greek oregano, for sprinkling
freshly ground black pepper
fresh oregano or continental parsley leaves, for garnish

Char capsicums on all sides directly over a gas flame or chargrill pan until blackened. Allow to cool.

Place onto serving plates and top with crumbled feta cheese, olives and a drizzling of oil.

Serve sprinkled with dried Greek oregano, pepper and fresh oregano leaves.

VARIATION Look out for long light green banana capsicums when they are in season.

TIPS
Roast capsicums will keep refrigerated for up to a week if you dress them with vinegar, oil and salt.

STYLING
Arrange the roast capsicums side by side and sprinkle the feta, olives and oregano across the middle before drizzling with oil.

DRINK MATCH
Riesling, sangiovese or crisp lager.

AUTUMN PASSIONS 115

Starter/Snack

Pistachio Crumbed Olives with Basil Mayo

Serves 4 • **Preparation time** 10 minutes • **Cooking time** 5 minutes

Pop one of these babies into your mouth at cocktail hour! You can easily make them ahead of time and keep them refrigerated, ready for a quick fry while the drinks are being shaken.

125g drained stuffed or pitted green olives
2 tablespoons plain flour
1 egg, lightly beaten
⅓ cup shelled pistachios, finely chopped
extra light olive oil or canola oil, for frying

BASIL MAYO
½ cup egg mayonnaise
2 tablespoons basil leaves, finely chopped

Toss olives in flour, dip in egg and coat in pistachio crumbs. Refrigerate for 10 minutes.

Just prior to serving, heat oil in a frypan and shallow fry olives until golden. Drain on paper towel and serve with Basil Mayo for dipping.

To make **Basil Mayo**, mix mayonnaise and basil together.

VARIATION Use unstuffed pitted green olives, cut in half lengthways. Fill with goat's cheese and sandwich back together before crumbing.

TIPS
Crumbed olives can be made and refrigerated 24 hours in advance, or frozen for up to 3 months and cooked from frozen.

STYLING
Use decorative cocktail sticks for serving, and garnish with small basil leaves.

DRINK MATCH
Prosecco, dry sherry, hefeweizen or saison.

Starter/Side

Roast Beetroot and Radicchio with Balsamic Glaze

Serves 4 • **Preparation time** 10 minutes • **Cooking time** 30 minutes

Underrated and underused, beetroot becomes less troublesome when it's roasted and sparked up with a vinegary dressing. Matched here with the grown up taste of radicchio and rare purple carrots, it's a salad that will turn heads at the table.

1 bunch baby beetroot
2 purple carrots (or regular carrots), scrubbed
1 red onion, cut into wedges
extra virgin olive oil, for drizzling
sea salt and pepper, to taste
1 radicchio
balsamic glaze, for drizzling
1 tablespoon chopped pistachio nuts

Trim the stalks of the beetroot, retaining the most tender leaves, and scrub well.

Place beetroot, carrots and onion wedges onto an oven tray; drizzle with oil and season. Roast at 200°C for 30 minutes until tender. Allow to cool.

Cut beetroot in half and slice carrots diagonally. Arrange on a bed of radicchio and beetroot leaves, together with roasted onion. Drizzle with oil and balsamic glaze, and serve sprinkled with pistachio nuts.

VARIATION Use spinach leaves or rocket if you don't love the bitterness of radicchio.

TIPS
Use tongs or gloves when cutting beetroot to avoid purple fingers!

STYLING
Chop the pistachio coarsely so the pop of green is more visible on the salad.

DRINK MATCH
Rosé or fruited sour ale.

Side

Sesame Carrots with Mandarin Juice

Serves 4-6 • **Preparation time** 10 minutes • **Cooking time** 20 minutes

Carrots will never be boring again if you roast them, spice them and dress them this way, with a squeeze of fresh mandarin or a juicy orange.

2 bunches Dutch carrots
extra virgin olive oil, for drizzling
sea salt and pepper, to taste
smoked paprika, for sprinkling
50g wild rocket
1 large mandarin or small orange, squeezed
2 teaspoons toasted sesame seeds

Trim the tops of the carrots and scrub well. Place onto an oven tray and drizzle with oil, sprinkle with salt and smoked paprika, and roast at 200°C for 20 minutes until tender.

Arrange rocket on a serving plate and top with roasted carrots.

Drizzle with mandarin juice and olive oil and serve sprinkled with sesame seeds and extra paprika.

VARIATION Use a sprinkling of dukkah instead of sesame seeds.

TIPS
Look out for the heirloom bunches of rainbow Dutch carrots that come in purple, orange, yellow and white.

STYLING
Keep the tops of the carrots on for a great look.

DRINK MATCH
Riesling or fruited sour ale.

Salad

Kipfler Potato, Radish and Pea Salad

Serves 4-6 • **Preparation time** 15 minutes • **Cooking time** 15 minutes

I can have potatoes any which way, and nutty kipflers are a favourite. Here I have added the bright pop of peas and the crunch of pretty pink radishes, together with a dill dressing to lighten up the dish. The cornichons were not included in the image, which is why they are listed as optional, but I do recommend you add them!

1kg potatoes, scrubbed (kipfler)
1 bunch radishes, finely sliced
2 spring onions, sliced diagonally
1 cup frozen peas, thawed
½ cup chopped cornichons or dill pickles (optional)

DILL DRESSING
½ cup chopped dill
1 cup extra virgin olive oil
⅓ cup red or white wine vinegar
2 teaspoons Dijon mustard
sea salt and pepper, to taste

Bring potatoes to the boil in a pot of salted water and simmer for 15 minutes until tender. Drain and cut into thick diagonal slices. While still warm, toss with half the Dill Dressing.

Toss in radishes, spring onions, peas and cornichons.

Place in a serving bowl, drizzle with remaining dressing and garnish with extra dill. May be served warm or cold.

For the **Dill Dressing,** shake all ingredients together in a jar until combined. Use as required.

VARIATION Baby potatoes can be used in place of kipflers.

TIPS
This salad is really ideal when the potatoes are tossed through the dressing while warm, to absorb those tangy flavours.

STYLING
Pick the smallest, feathery tips of the dill first and reserve them for dropping delicately over the salad just prior to serving.

DRINK MATCH
Chardonnay or Australian pale ale.

Main

Cioppino Seafood Stew and Parmesan Garlic Rolls

Serves 6 • Preparation time 20 minutes • Cooking time 15 minutes

This Ligurian dish became popular on the docks of San Francisco, where Italian immigrant fisherman would pool their leftover catch together into a pot to make this tomato-based seafood stew (Cioppino is said to come from the Ligurian word for 'chopped'). This is my version and once you have prepared the seafood, cooking takes minutes. The crusty parmesan rolls are just what you need to soak up those irresistible juices.

500g mussels
200g salmon fillet
300g firm white fish fillets (eg Spanish mackerel, blue eye)
375g green prawn meat
250g scallops with roe
500g calamari rings
extra virgin olive oil, as needed
1 onion, finely diced
3 cloves garlic, crushed
2 large ripe tomatoes, diced
½ cup white or light red wine
1 cup tomato passata
¼ teaspoon chilli flakes
½ cup parsley leaves
sea salt and pepper, to taste

PARMESAN GARLIC ROLLS
100g softened butter
2 cloves garlic, crushed
1 tablespoon chopped parsley
½ cup grated parmesan
6 round bread rolls

To prepare the seafood, debeard and scrub the mussels. Cut the fish fillets into 2cm cubes. Remove the side muscle from the scallops.

To make the stew, heat ¼ cup oil in a large pot and sauté onion and garlic until softened. Add tomatoes, wine, passata and chilli flakes and simmer for 5 minutes until slightly thickened. Add mussels, cover and simmer for 5 minutes until they open. Add all the remaining seafood and simmer, stirring for 5 minutes until just cooked. Mix in parsley, season and serve with Parmesan Garlic Rolls.

To make **Parmesan Garlic Rolls**, combine butter, garlic, parsley and parmesan together. Cut deep vertical slits into each roll, spread with butter and bake at 200°C for 10 minutes until rolls are crisp and butter has melted.

VARIATION To make a delicious Spaghetti Marinara, simply toss cooked spaghetti through the finished Cioppino.

TIPS
Make the sauce in advance and add the seafood to cook just before serving.

STYLING
Position the mussels facing upwards in the serving bowl and finish with parsley leaves.

DRINK MATCH
Montepulciano d'Abruzzo or farmhouse ale.

AUTUMN PASSIONS 127

Main
Moroccan Chicken Pie (*B'stilla*)

Serves 4-6 • **Preparation time** 20 minutes • **Cooking time** 25 minutes

This majestic Moroccan pie lifts hearts when it comes to the table. For me, it evokes memories of wandering through the Marrakech spice markets and watching the stall vendors expertly making the delicate warqa pastry before my eyes. I use readily available filo instead, and although B'stilla (pronounced pas-ti-ya) was first made using pigeon, a roast chook does the trick!

⅓ cup toasted slivered almonds
1 teaspoon cinnamon
2 teaspoons icing sugar
¼ teaspoon saffron threads
sea salt
1 cup boiling water
2 tablespoons olive oil
1 large red onion, finely sliced
2 cloves garlic, crushed
2 teaspoons ras el hanout (Moroccan spice mix)
1 teaspoon honey
1 roast chicken, deboned and shredded
2 eggs, lightly beaten
½ cup chopped coriander or continental parsley
8 sheets filo pastry
60g butter, melted
icing sugar and cinnamon, for sprinkling

Blend almonds, cinnamon and icing sugar together in a nut mill or crush in a mortar and pestle, to a fine powder. Add saffron and 1 teaspoon salt to boiling water and stand.

Heat oil in a large frypan and sauté onion and garlic until softened. Add ras el hanout and honey and sauté for 1 minute. Add saffron water, bring to the boil and simmer until reduced by half. Add shredded chicken and cook until heated through. Stir in eggs until just scrambled. Cool slightly and stir in coriander.

Brush filo sheets with butter. Lay into a 20-22cm round springform tin, rotating and overlapping the pastry as you go, and letting the pastry overhang the tin. Spoon the chicken filling into the tin and top with almond mixture. Gather up the overhanging pastry to cover the filling and brush with melted butter.

Bake at 200°C for 20-25 minutes until golden. Allow to cool for 5 minutes before removing from the tin. Serve sprinkled with a little icing sugar and cinnamon.

VARIATION The filling can be used to make individual filo triangles instead. Brush each sheet, fold in half lengthways, spoon filling onto one end and fold up into a triangle, folding continually up the length of the pastry.

TIPS
The pie can be made up to 2 hours in advance and reheated before serving.

STYLING
Drape the overhanging pastry into folds as you are covering the top of the pie, so it has a ruffled appearance.

DRINK MATCH
Riesling, pinot noir, crisp lager or amber ale.

Main

Polenta-crumbed Flathead with Caper Mayonnaise on Garlic Mash

Serves 4 • **Preparation time** 10 minutes • **Cooking time** 10 minutes

Crumbing fish with polenta creates a crunchy crumb that is never oily. It turns Friday fish and chips into a restaurant-quality dish!

1 cup polenta
2 teaspoons turmeric
½ teaspoon chilli powder
sea salt and pepper, to taste
800g flathead fillets, cut into pieces
¼ cup extra light olive oil, for frying
lemon wedges, for serving

GARLIC MASH

750g potatoes (Dutch creams or similar)
3 garlic cloves, peeled
⅓ cup extra virgin olive oil

SAUTÉED SPINACH

1 tablespoon olive oil
80g baby spinach leaves, washed
1 tablespoon chopped dill

LEMON CAPER MAYONNAISE

1 cup egg mayonnaise
2 teaspoons Dijon mustard
1 tablespoon baby capers
1 tablespoon chopped dill
grated rind of 1 lemon
1 tablespoon lemon juice

Combine polenta, turmeric, chilli and 1 teaspoon salt together. Coat fish in polenta crumbs. Heat oil in a frypan and pan fry fish for 2-3 minutes on each side until golden. Drain on absorbent paper and serve on a bed of Garlic Potato Mash and Sautéed Spinach with Lemon Caper Mayonnaise and lemon.

For the **Garlic Mas**h, peel potatoes, cut in half and bring to the boil in a large saucepan of salted water. Add garlic cloves and boil for 20-30 minutes until very tender. Drain and mash potatoes and garlic together until very smooth. Slowly mix in olive oil and season to taste.

For the **Sautéed Spinach,** heat oil and sauté spinach and dill in a saucepan until just wilted. Season.

For the **Lemon Caper Mayonnaise,** combine all ingredients together and season to taste.

VARIATION Chicken tenderloins or slices of tofu can be crumbed in the same way.

TIPS
Fish can be crumbed and refrigerated up to 24 hours before cooking. Mash also reheats very well.

STYLING
Spread waves of mash onto the plate with the back of a spoon, top with spinach and fish, and finish with mayonnaise, dill and capers.

DRINK MATCH
Riesling or Australian pale ale.

Main

Persian Chicken Pilaf

Serves 6 • **Preparation time** 15 minutes • **Cooking time** 45 minutes

If only you could smell the heady spices in this dish as you read the recipe, then you would be certain to try it. Lavishly decorated with jewels of pomegranate, toasted nuts and mint leaves, when it comes to the table, it will impress everyone.

1¼ cups basmati or long grain rice
¼ cup pine nuts
extra virgin olive oil, as needed
1 large onion, thinly sliced
sea salt and pepper, to taste
6 chicken thighs*
50g butter
pomegranate molasses, for drizzling
¼ cup pomegranate seeds
¼ cup mint leaves, for garnish

AROMATIC STOCK
1 litre chicken stock
⅓ cup currants
2 slices lemon
2 bay leaves
1 cinnamon stick
6 cardamom pods, split
1 teaspoon allspice
¼ teaspoon saffron threads or 1 teaspoon turmeric

Rinse rice in a sieve until water runs clear and allow to drain. Combine all the ingredients for the **Aromatic Stock** in a saucepan and bring to the boil. Turn off the heat and allow to infuse.

Dry-fry pine nuts in a large wide ovenproof pan until golden and remove. Heat 2 tablespoons oil in the pan, add onion, season and fry until golden brown and remove. Season chicken well and sear in the pan until golden brown on both sides, adding more oil if needed. It doesn't need to be cooked through at this stage. Remove.

Melt butter and 1 tablespoon oil in pan and fry rice until opaque. Add hot Aromatic Stock and bring to the boil. Place chicken pieces on top, reduce heat and simmer covered for 15 minutes. Turn off and allow to stand covered for another 15 minutes until rice has absorbed the liquid.

Serve sprinkled with fried onions, pine nuts, a drizzle of pomegranate molasses, pomegranate seeds and mint leaves.

VARIATION For a vegetarian option, use 1 large eggplant, cut into wedges, instead of chicken. Salt eggplant and allow to stand for 10 minutes before frying in oil, as above, instead of chicken.

TIPS
*Use unskinned chicken thighs with the bone in for best flavour.

STYLING
Spoon rice and chicken onto a large platter, then layer with onions, pine nuts, pomegranate seeds and tiny mint leaves.

DRINK MATCH
Riesling, merlot or Australian pale ale.

Main

Seared Duck Breast with Pinot Grapes and Duck Fat Potatoes

Serves 4 • **Preparation time** 20 minutes • **Cooking time** 30 minutes

This is my daughter's favourite dinner, created for her birthday one year - perfectly pink duck breast with wine-soaked grapes and crispy duck fat potatoes. Delicious with a glass of pinot.

3 large potatoes, peeled (Dutch cream, royal blue or desiree)
4 duck breasts*
sea salt and pepper, to taste
cinnamon, for sprinkling
1 bunch fresh thyme
extra virgin olive oil, for drizzling

PINOT GRAPES
1 cup pinot noir wine
½ cup dark brown sugar
1 cinnamon stick
piece of orange peel
250g dark red grapes

THREE PEAS
150g snow peas, trimmed
150g sugar snap peas, trimmed
½ cup frozen peas, thawed
50g butter
sea salt, to taste
1 teaspoon grated orange rind

Boil potatoes in salted water for 15-20 minutes until just tender, drain and dice. Score the skin of the duck breasts with a sharp knife and pat dry with paper towel. Sprinkle all over with salt, and sprinkle the underside with a little cinnamon. Cook in a frypan, skin side down, for 10-15 minutes until skin is crisp and golden. Brown briefly on the second side. Keeping the duck fat in the frypan, remove duck onto a bed of thyme on an oven tray and roast at 200°C for 5 minutes, then rest for 5 minutes before serving. Meanwhile, fry diced potatoes and 1 tablespoon chopped thyme in duck fat over high heat, cooking until golden, and season.

To serve, place a nest of potatoes on the centre of each serving plate. Top with sliced duck with Pinot Grapes on the side. Drizzle with pinot syrup and a little olive oil. Garnish with thyme and serve with Three Peas.

For the **Pinot Grapes**, simmer wine, sugar, cinnamon stick, orange peel and a few sprigs of thyme for 5-10 minutes until syrupy. Just before serving, add grapes in small bunches, simmer for 5 minutes and season.

For the **Three Peas**, place all peas in a frypan with 1 cup water and cook until just tender, but still bright green. Refresh in cold water and drain. Melt butter in a frypan, then add peas and orange rind and toss until heated through. Season.

TIPS
*If the duck breasts come with the wing attached, remove them.

STYLING
Fan the sliced duck over potatoes.

DRINK MATCH
Pinot noir or hazy pale ale.

AUTUMN PASSIONS

Main
Eggplant Involtini with Tomato Capsicum Sauce

Serves 4 • **Preparation time** 30 minutes • **Cooking time** 30 minutes

This Sicilian classic is my all-time favourite eggplant dish and it just happens to suit every vegetarian I know too. Assemble it in advance, and then just give it a blast in the oven to deliciously meld everything together and turn it into a feel-good dish that rivals lasagne.

2 large eggplants
extra virgin olive oil, as needed
sea salt and pepper, to taste
¼ cup pine nuts
2 cloves garlic, crushed
1 cup finely chopped, crustless stale bread
500g full-fat ricotta (cut from the wheel)
½ cup chopped fresh basil
1 cup grated provolone*

TOMATO CAPSICUM SAUCE
1 tablespoon olive oil
1 onion, finely chopped
1 small red capsicum, finely chopped
½ cup wine or stock
400g can peeled tomatoes
sugar, to taste

Cut eggplants lengthwise into 12 thin slices (½ cm thick). Brush with oil, season with salt and grill or chargrill on one side only. Dry-fry the pine nuts in a frypan until golden and remove. Heat 1 tablespoon oil in the frypan and fry garlic, bread and 1 teaspoon salt until toasted. Break up the ricotta using a fork; add the pine nuts, toasted bread mixture and basil, mixing with your hand. Season to taste.

Divide the ricotta filling evenly between eggplant slices, placing the filling on the short end of the eggplant and rolling up to enclose. Pour Tomato Capsicum Sauce into the base of a lasagne dish, nestle the eggplant involtini into the sauce, sprinkle with provolone and bake at 200°C for 30 minutes until golden brown. Serve sprinkled with basil leaves and extra toasted pine nuts.

For the **Tomato Capsicum Sauce**, heat olive oil in a frypan and sauté onion and capsicum until softened. Add wine and chopped tomatoes and simmer for 5-10 minutes until thickened. Season to taste, adding a little sugar if needed.

*****VARIATION** Provolone can be substituted for half mozzarella, half parmesan.

TIPS
This dish can be fully assembled and refrigerated up to 24 hours in advance.

STYLING
Roll the eggplant with the chargrilled side out to show the grill marks.

DRINK MATCH
Riesling, shiraz or Italian pilsner

Main

Swiss Brown Mushroom and Gruyère Tart

Serves 6 • **Preparation time** 15 minutes • **Cooking time** 20 minutes

Puff pastry sheets in the freezer are my standby to create easy-bake pastry tarts and let my imagination run wild with the toppings. This stunning savoury mushroom tart with the sweet undertones of gruyère is just the thing for an autumn table.

50g butter
4 golden shallots or 1 large onion, thinly sliced
500g Swiss brown mushrooms, sliced
sea salt and pepper, to taste
375g sheet frozen puff pastry*, thawed
1 cup grated gruyère or vintage cheddar cheese
1 tablespoon fresh thyme leaves, plus extra for garnish
extra virgin olive oil, for drizzling

Melt half the butter in a frypan. Sauté shallots until softened and remove. Melt remaining butter and sauté mushrooms until lightly browned, then season and allow to cool.

Place pastry on an oven tray and score a 1cm border around the edges using a sharp knife. Prick the base with a fork. Top with cheese, shallots, mushrooms and thyme and sprinkle with pepper.

Bake in the upper half of the oven at 200°C for 15 minutes, then lower to the base of the oven for 5 minutes to crisp the underside of the pastry.

Drizzle with olive oil and serve garnished with extra thyme.

VARIATION Try with thinly sliced zucchini and halved cherry tomatoes, instead of mushrooms.

TIPS
*Carême puff pastry was used in this recipe. If unavailable, substitute 2 standard puff pastry sheets and place them on top of each other to make a square tart.

STYLING
Serve tart whole, drizzled with olive oil and sprinkled with fresh thyme sprigs.

DRINK MATCH
Pinot noir or American strong ale.

AUTUMN PASSIONS

Main/Starter

Homemade Gnocchi with Wild Mushroom Sauce

Serves 6 as main, 8 as a starter • **Preparation time** 1 hour • **Cooking time** 20 minutes

Therapeutic in the making and the eating, gnocchi always brings the family together. We have had many plates of hand-rolled gnocchi at my mum-in-law's table over the years, served with her famous polpette on the side. This is my version with a very sensuous wild mushroom sauce that is my pasta-loving son's fave.

1kg potatoes, unpeeled, scrubbed
sea salt and pepper, to taste
1 large egg
200-300g plain flour, as needed
30g dried wild mushrooms (chanterelle, porcini or forest mushrooms)
50g butter
4 spring onions, chopped
4 cloves garlic, crushed
400g Swiss brown mushrooms, sliced
1 cup dry white wine
fresh thyme
300ml pure cream
½ cup grated parmesan and extra for serving

For the gnocchi, boil unpeeled potatoes whole in a large pot of salted water until very soft in the centre. Press warm potatoes through a potato ricer onto a floured bench top, discarding the skins or peel and mash with a fork. Make a well in the centre of the riced potato, add the egg and mix by hand. Slowly mix in just enough flour to make a soft dough, kneading very gently until the mixture is smooth. The dough should be slightly springy but not as elastic as a bread dough. Divide dough into 6 pieces and roll each into a long rope, around 2cm thick. Cut into 3 cm pieces and, using your finger tip, gently roll each piece to dimple it. Arrange on a large floured tray as you roll the gnocchi, flouring lightly as you go. Cook gnocchi in a large pot of boiling salted water until all the gnocchi rise to the surface. Drain and cover to keep warm while making sauce.

For the **Wild Mushroom Sauce**, cover dried mushrooms with 1 cup boiling water and stand until soft. Chop into large pieces with scissors. Melt butter in pot and sauté spring onions, garlic and Swiss brown mushrooms until softened. Add wine, soaked mushrooms and their liquid and a few sprigs of thyme. Bring to the boil and simmer until reduced by one third. Add cream and simmer until saucy. Stir in parmesan and season.

To serve, stir gnocchi into the hot sauce. Serve garnished with extra thyme and parmesan.

TIPS
It's best to use old potatoes as they tend to be more floury.

STYLING
Use a vegetable peeler to shave parmesan into flakes.

DRINK MATCH
Chardonnay or Italian pilsner.

AUTUMN PASSIONS 143

Main

Chicken, Chorizo and Sundried Tomato Risotto

Serves 4 • **Preparation time** 10 minutes • **Cooking time** 30 minutes

This is what happens when risotto meets paella! Truth be told, I think this recipe evolved from leftover ingredients I had in the fridge, but it has become a family favourite due to its rich colour and flavour.

500g skinned boneless chicken thighs, diced
sea salt and pepper, to taste
100g sundried tomato strips in oil, drained, oil reserved
1 red onion, diced
1 cup arborio rice
2 cloves garlic, crushed
200g chorizo, sliced
1.5 litres hot chicken stock
50g butter, cubed
2 tablespoons continental parsley leaves
grated parmesan or manchego cheese, for serving

Season chicken. Heat reserved oil from the sundried tomato in a large pan and brown seasoned chicken for 5 minutes until just cooked. Remove and keep warm.

Add onion to pan and sauté until softened. Add rice and cook stirring until rice is opaque. Add garlic and chorizo and brown. Add sundried tomatoes and half the simmering stock and cook uncovered, stirring until all the liquid has been absorbed. Continue adding stock 1 cup at a time, stirring regularly, until the rice is cooked to al dente stage - this will take 15-20 minutes.

Just before serving, stir in diced chicken, butter and parsley. Serve risotto in bowls sprinkled with cheese and garnish with extra parsley if desired.

VARIATION Italian sausage or chopped salami can be used in place of chorizo.

TIPS
Always use arborio, carnaroli or vialone nano rice for making risotto.

STYLING
Risotto is best served in a wide, flat, scooped bowl so that you get a little parmesan garnish in every forkful.

DRINK MATCH
Tempranillo, sangiovese, amber ale or session IPA.

Main
Turkish Lamb Pide

Serves 8 • **Preparation time** 1½ hours (including standing time) • **Cooking time** 20 minutes

These hand-rolled pide take a little time, but they are worth mastering because once you have the dough you can fill them with anything. Spiced lamb makes them a meal in your hand and perfect for picnicking. I have also included a vegetarian-friendly spinach, feta and pine nut filling.

5 cups plain flour, plus extra
sea salt
¾ cup milk
¾ cup water
2 teaspoons dried yeast
1 teaspoon sugar
2 eggs
80g softened butter
500g lamb mince
1 red onion, finely diced
1 tablespoon ground cumin
2 tablespoons finely chopped coriander
3 tomatoes, finely diced
2 tablespoons pine nuts
dried chilli flakes and coriander leaves, for garnish
180g marinated feta or natural yoghurt, for serving

Combine flour and 2 teaspoons salt in a large bowl. Heat milk and water until just lukewarm. Make a well in the centre of the flour, add the milk mixture and stir in the yeast and sugar. Add eggs and butter and mix to a dough with your hand, adding extra flour if required. Knead for 5 minutes until smooth and elastic. Cover and stand in a warm place for 30 minutes.*

Knock back dough and divide into 8. Roll out into long oval shapes, 5mm thick.

Combine mince, onion, cumin, coriander and 1 teaspoon salt with ½ cup tomato. Divide evenly along each piece of dough, leaving a border. Sprinkle with pine nuts and chilli flakes. Turn in the edges and twist ends to form a 'boat' shape. Place on oven trays and bake at 220°C for 20 minutes until golden brown.

Top with diced tomatoes, marinated feta or dollops of yoghurt and coriander leaves.

VARIATION Spinach, Feta and Pine Nut filling: Sauté 250g spinach leaves until wilted, squeeze out excess moisture. Add 200g crumbled feta, 3 chopped spring onions, 2 tablespoons toasted pine nuts and 2 eggs.

TIPS
*When proving the dough, place it in a sunny spot, near a central heating vent or on the open door of the oven while it is preheating.

STYLING
Arrange on a big board and garnish each one with tomato, feta, coriander and chilli flakes just before serving.

DRINK MATCH
Shiraz or hazy IPA.

Main
Roast Pumpkin Rotolo

Serves 8 • **Preparation time** 30 minutes • **Cooking time** 30 minutes

So much less fiddly than making ravioli and much more impressive in looks, a rotolo is my kind of filled pasta. The only tricky bit is finding some muslin to wrap it up into a bon-bon shape, ready for poaching. Once you master the technique, the filling choice is all yours – spinach, mushroom, pea, beetroot, sweet potato... shall I go on?

1kg pumpkin, peeled and diced
extra virgin olive oil, as needed
sea salt and pepper, to taste
2 spring onions, chopped
750g fresh full-fat ricotta, cut from the wheel
1 bunch basil leaves, chopped (reserve some leaves for garnish)
1 egg, lightly beaten
375g (8 sheets) fresh lasagne sheets
milk, for brushing
200g butter, cubed
toasted pine nuts, for garnish
grated parmesan, for serving
4 x 30cm square pieces of muslin/cheesecloth
kitchen string

Place pumpkin on an oven tray. Drizzle with oil and season. Roast at 200°C, in the top of the oven or under a grill, for 15 minutes or until golden brown and tender. Mash with a fork and mix in spring onions, ricotta, half the basil and egg, and season.

Place two lasagne sheets next to each other on a piece of muslin, with long edges overlapping by 5cm to form a large rectangle. Brush with milk and spread with a quarter of the ricotta mixture, leaving a border along the far long edge. Using the muslin, roll up the lasagne to form a roll, enclosing the filling and wrapping the muslin firmly around the roll. Tie the ends securely with kitchen string. Repeat with remaining lasagne sheets and filling to form four rolls.

Cook rolls in a deep roasting pan of boiling salted water for 25-30 minutes. Remove, unwrap, cut into slices and spoon over Basil Butter Sauce. Garnish with pine nuts and reserved basil leaves. Serve with parmesan cheese.

For **Basil Butter Sauce**, just before serving, melt butter until hot, then add remaining basil and cook until butter just starts to colour, taking care not to burn it. Serve over sliced rotolo.

TIPS
Choose thin pasta sheets, or if they are thicker, parboil for 1 minute beforehand. Assembled rotolo may be kept refrigerated for 24 hours in advance.

STYLING
Stand the cut slices of rotolo upright before pouring the butter sauce over them, and sprinkling with pine nuts and basil leaves.

DRINK MATCH
Soave, chardonnay, Italian pilsner or pumpkin ale.

Main

Gruyère Chicken with French Onion Sauce and Paris Mash

Serves 6 • **Preparation time** 10 minutes • **Cooking time** 45 minutes

This bistro-style dish with French onion sauce evolved from the classic French onion soup you will find in any Parisian bistro. It's delicious with a rich mash that is definitely worth the effort to make it.

6 chicken breast fillets, skinned
sea salt and pepper, to taste
100g butter
4 large brown onions, sliced
4 cloves garlic, crushed
¼ cup brandy
1 cup beef stock
1 tablespoon Dijon mustard
½ bunch fresh thyme sprigs
250g gruyère, raclette or tilsit, sliced

PARIS MASH
600g medium potatoes, unpeeled (Dutch cream or desiree)
sea salt, to taste
¾ cup milk
200g chilled unsalted butter, cubed

Season chicken fillets. Melt 20g butter in a large frypan, brown chicken fillets on both sides, and remove. Melt remaining butter and cook onions over low heat, stirring occasionally, for 30 minutes until caramelised. Add garlic and sauté over high heat for 1 minute. Flambé pan with brandy, then add stock, mustard and half the thyme sprigs. Return chicken to pan and simmer covered for 10 minutes until cooked through. Top each fillet with cheese and simmer covered for 5 minutes until cheese has melted. Serve sprinkled with pepper and remaining thyme.

For the **Paris Mash**, scrub the potatoes well. Place in a saucepan, cover with water and add 1 teaspoon salt. Bring to the boil and boil for 30 minutes or until the potatoes are very soft in the centre when tested with a skewer. Peel and mash the hot potatoes until very smooth. Return potatoes to the clean saucepan and heat, stirring with a wooden spoon to remove excess moisture. Heat half the milk and add to the mash, together with 50g butter. Pass the mash through a fine sieve back into the saucepan - this is optional but results in a super smooth mash. Just prior to serving, reheat and mix in enough butter and remaining hot milk to make a rich, creamy mash that is your desired consistency. Season and serve with chicken.

TIPS
The chicken can be browned and the sauce can be made in advance before finishing off the cooking just before serving. The Paris Mash also reheats very well.

STYLING
To get a little more browning on the gruyère, finish it off under the grill.

DRINK MATCH
Chardonnay, pinot noir, amber ale or German dunkel.

AUTUMN PASSIONS

Main

Chicken Scaloppine with Marsala Mushrooms and Soft Polenta

Serves 4 • **Preparation time** 10 minutes • **Cooking time** 15 minutes

This Italian bistro dish was the recipe of choice for my very first virtual Cook-Along class, and I think it is something that everyone should know how to make. Served over a soft, buttery polenta, it is one of my husband's favourite meals.

2 large chicken fillets, skinned
1 bunch sage, thyme or rosemary
sea salt and pepper, to taste
1 tablespoon olive oil
50g butter
1 onion, finely chopped
200g Swiss brown mushrooms, sliced
1 cup marsala or white wine
½ cup cream

SOFT POLENTA
2 cups chicken or beef stock
½ cup polenta
50g butter
sea salt, to taste

Remove the tenderloin from each chicken fillet. Cut the rest of the fillets in half horizontally. Place all chicken pieces on a layer of plastic wrap, season well and press a few sage leaves onto each piece. Cover with another layer of plastic wrap. Using a rolling pin, gently batten out to even thickness.

Heat the oil and butter in a frypan and brown the chicken on both sides. Remove.

Sauté the onion in the pan until translucent, then add the mushrooms and sauté until softened. Add the marsala, cream and 1 tablespoon chopped sage leaves to the pan and simmer until thickened. Season to taste. Return chicken to the pan to cook through.

Serve over Soft Polenta garnished with extra sage leaves.

To make **Soft Polenta**, bring stock to the boil, whisk in polenta and cook, stirring over medium heat, until thickened. Allow to stand covered for 5 minutes, stir in butter and season to taste. If polenta thickens too much, adjust with a little boiling water.

TIPS
The soft polenta will firm up on cooling, so be sure to serve it as soon as it is ready.

STYLING
Smear the polenta onto the plate so it will catch the sauce, and position the chicken on top before saucing.

DRINK MATCH
Pinot grigio or American pale ale.

AUTUMN PASSIONS 153

Lunch
Mighty Muffuletta

Serves 4 • **Preparation time** 15 minutes (plus 30 min standing)

The muffuletta is surely one of the world's greatest sandwiches. I have fond memories of getting our taxi to stop at Central Grocery and Deli in New Orleans on our way to the airport to pick one up before we left that vibrant city. This layered wonder is perfect picnic food and it's worth making extra olive salad to keep in the fridge, for sandwich emergencies!

1 round Italian-style loaf of bread*
extra virgin olive oil, for drizzling
100g thinly sliced smoked ham
100g thinly sliced sopressa
100g thinly sliced mortadella
150g thinly sliced provolone cheese
¼ cup continental parsley leaves
freshly ground black pepper, to taste

OLIVE SALAD

350g jar Giardiniera mixed pickles & vinegar, chopped
1 cup green pitted olives, chopped
1 cup pitted black kalamata olives, chopped
2 tablespoons capers
4 cloves garlic, chopped
½ cup extra virgin olive oil

Cut a circle of bread off the top of the bread loaf and hollow out the centre (you can use this to make fresh breadcrumbs). Drizzle both sides of the bread with olive oil and some of the Olive Salad vinegar.

Place ½ cup Olive Salad inside the bread shell and layer with ham, sopressa, mortadella, provolone, remaining Olive Salad and parsley leaves. Season with pepper and place bread lid on top.

Wrap and weigh down with a heavy weight for at least 30 minutes to compress the sandwich. Serve cut into quarters.

For **Olive Salad**, combine all ingredients together and store refrigerated until required (for up to one month).

*****VARIATION** Instead of one large loaf, use hollowed out round rolls to make individual-serve muffulettas.

TIPS
Use a sharp serrated bread knife to gently saw through the layers when cutting the muffuletta.

STYLING
Take care in pressing down each ingredient inside the bread loaf, to achieve the layered effect.

DRINK MATCH
Rioja, lambrusco or Australian pale ale.

Winter comforts

Light the fire and the oven so
the slow cooked aromas warm the
bones of the house and the soul.

Comforting mouthfuls of rich
flavours and deep colours tempt
us at the table like
the warmest of hugs.

Come inside and cocoon over food
that speaks to the heart.

TASTE*ful*

WINTER COMFORTS 159

Starter/Dip

Hot Parmesan and Artichoke Dip with Sesame Cumin Crisps

Serves 6 · Preparation time 10 minutes **· Cooking time** 20 minutes

A warm, wintery dip that can be mixed up ahead of time and heated just before serving, with crunchy pita crisps on the side. It's worth having some canned artichokes in the pantry to reach for, just for this purpose.

60g parmesan cheese
200g artichoke hearts in brine, drained and quartered
1 clove garlic, crushed
½ cup egg mayonnaise
1 teaspoon Dijon mustard
2 teaspoons lemon juice
1 tablespoon chopped continental parsley
paprika or cayenne pepper, for sprinkling

SESAME CUMIN CRISPS
1 tablespoon sesame seeds
2 teaspoons ground cumin
1 teaspoon sea salt flakes
2 pita breads, split in half
olive oil, for brushing

Finely grate parmesan cheese and combine with artichoke hearts, garlic, mayonnaise, mustard and lemon juice in a saucepan.

Just prior to serving, cook, stirring continuously until cheese melts and dip is hot. Stir in parsley, spoon into a serving bowl and sprinkle with paprika.

Serve hot with Sesame Cumin Crisps.

For the **Sesame Cumin Crisps**, combine sesame, cumin and sea salt. Brush pita breads with olive oil and sprinkle with spice mix. Cut into wedges and bake on an oven tray at 200°C for 5-10 minutes until crisp and golden. Allow to cool and store in an airtight container.

VARIATION For a vegan version, use vegan mayonnaise and replace the parmesan cheese with ¼ cup finely chopped green olives.

TIPS
Make ahead and reheat in the saucepan just prior to serving.

STYLING
Keep some artichoke halves for garnish, ruffling the leaves with your fingers to make them flower-like.

DRINK MATCH
Sparkling, pinot grigio or American pale ale.

WINTER COMFORTS

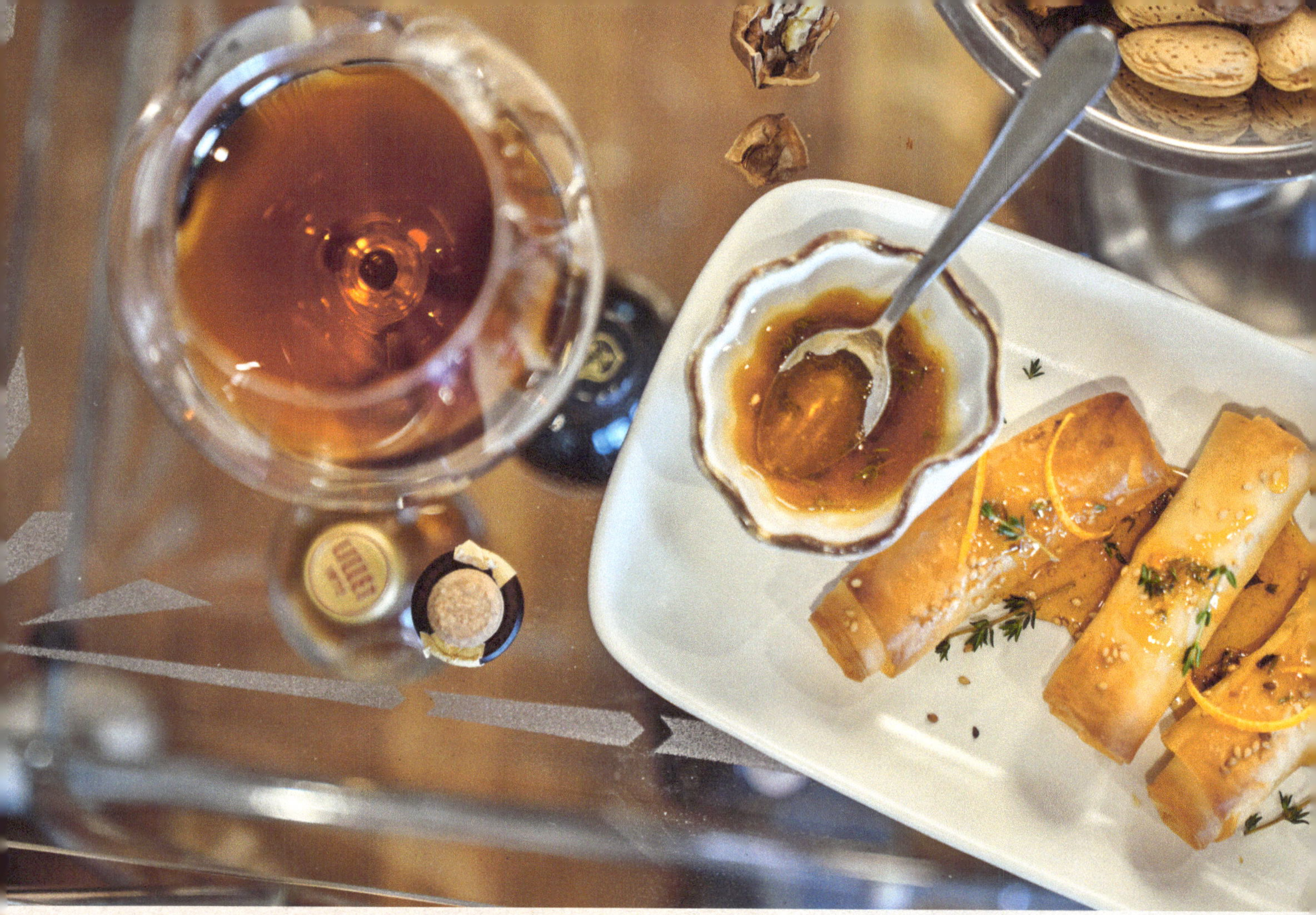

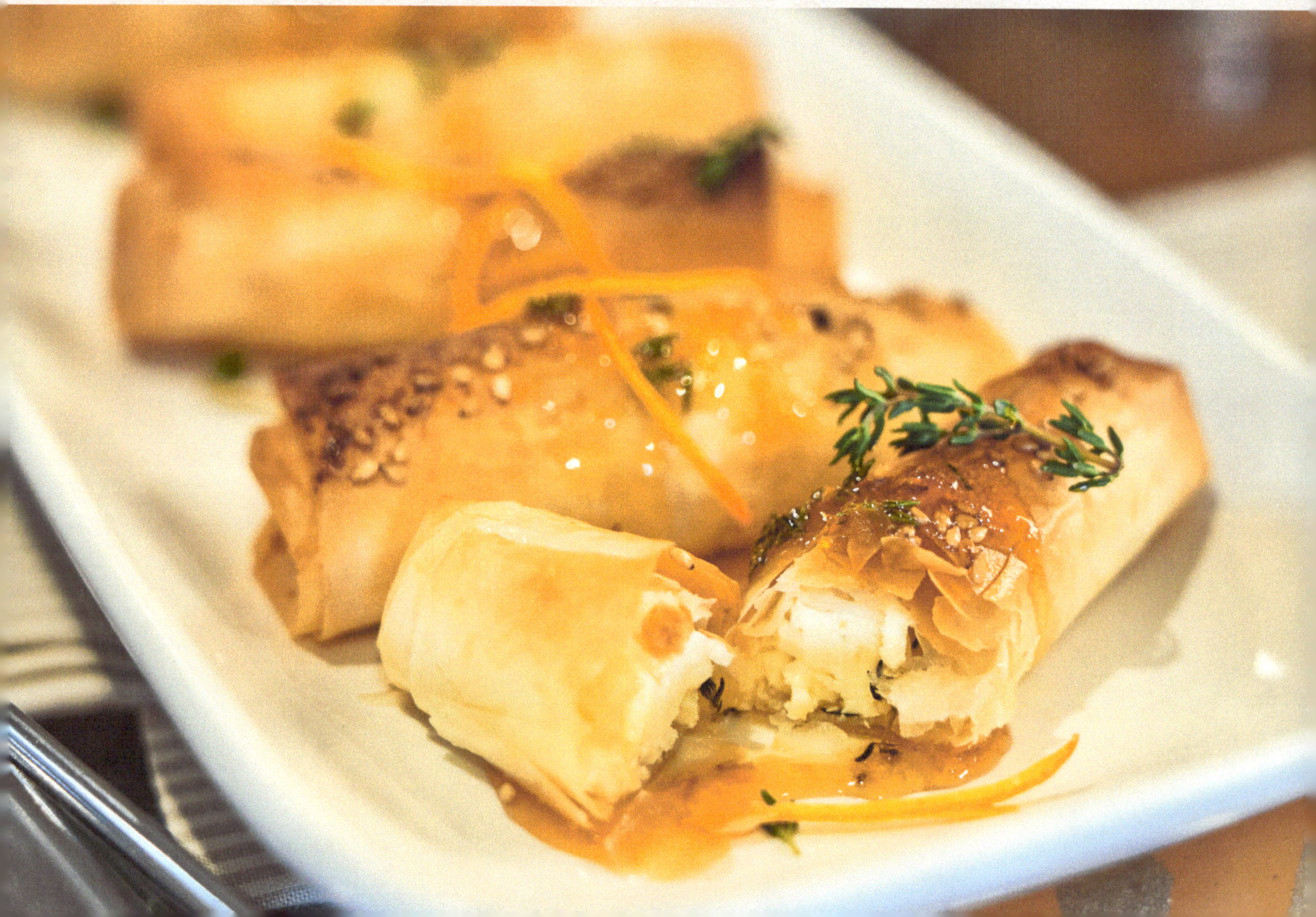

Starter/Snack

Feta Cigars with Mandarin and Thyme Honey

Makes 12 • **Preparation time** 15 minutes • **Cooking time** 10 minutes

These delectable little filo rolls with a creamy feta centre are doused in a citrus honey and are impossible to resist. Assemble them up to a day ahead and bake them just before serving for the ultimate pre-dinner snack.

200g feta cheese
6 sheets filo pastry
50g butter, melted
sesame or poppy seeds, for sprinkling
1 bunch thyme
¼ cup honey
grated rind and juice of 1 mandarin (or ½ orange)

Cut the feta into 12 equal batons. Working quickly, cut each filo sheet in half lengthwise. Brush each piece with butter and place a feta baton and a sprig of thyme on the short end. Roll up into cigar shapes, folding in the sides as you go.

Place on an oven tray, brush with butter and sprinkle with seeds. Bake at 200°C in the upper half of the oven for 10 minutes until golden brown.

Meanwhile, warm honey on the stove with grated rind, 2 tablespoons of mandarin juice and a few thyme sprigs for a few minutes. Allow to cool to infuse the flavours.

Serve hot feta cigars drizzled with scented honey and sprinkled with thyme.

VARIATION Use batons of salted tofu and olive oil in place of butter for a vegan version.

TIPS
Uncooked feta cigars may be refrigerated, covered, for 24 hours before baking. They also freeze well. If cooking them from frozen, allow a few extra minutes.

STYLING
Spoon cooled honey over hot feta cigars just before serving, and sprinkle with orange rind and thyme leaves.

DRINK MATCH
Sauvignon blanc, riesling, cognac or Australian pale ale.

Starter/Snack
Cannellini Crostini

Makes 24 • **Preparation time** 5 minutes • **Cooking time** 15 minutes

Elegant and easy, these crunchy crostini topped with a creamy cannellini bean puree and crowned with a little tomato are perfect to serve with drinks. They are particularly good with a martini!

400g cannellini beans or butter beans, undrained
extra virgin olive oil, as needed
sea salt and pepper, to taste
125g semi dried tomatoes or 12 cherry tomatoes, halved

GREMOLATA
1 large clove garlic, peeled
2 tablespoons continental parsley leaves
grated rind of 1 lemon

Bring beans, together with their liquid, to the boil. Then reduce heat and simmer for 10 minutes, stirring occasionally, until creamy and most of the liquid has reduced. Mash with a fork. Stir in 1 tablespoon olive oil and season.

Cut baguette into approximately 24 thin slices. Brush with oil on both sides and grill until golden on both sides.

Spread with cannellini puree, top with a semi-dried tomato and serve drizzled with olive oil and sprinkled with Gremolata and pepper.

For the **Gremolata**, finely chop garlic and parsley together and mix in lemon rind.

VARIATION Chickpeas, butter beans or red kidney beans can be used in place of cannellini beans.

TIPS
Cannellini bean puree can be made in advance and gently warmed before assembling.

STYLING
Scatter the Gremolata across the serving plate for a fun, casual look.

DRINK MATCH
Chardonnay, pinot noir, martini or Italian pilsner.

WINTER COMFORTS

Starter

Mussel, Celery and Potato Chowder with Mustard Toasts

Serves 4 • **Preparation time** 20 minutes • **Cooking time** 40 minutes

Inspired by the clam chowder I had at San Francisco's Fisherman's Wharf, this mussel chowder emerged from my winter kitchen one day. It partners so well with these tasty little pieces of toast.

1kg mussels, scrubbed and debearded
2 litres fish stock*
2 tablespoons olive oil
1 leek or large onion, finely chopped
2 stalks celery and leaves, finely diced
50g butter
½ cup flour
750g potatoes, peeled, finely diced (Dutch creams)
½ cup cream
sea salt and pepper, to taste
cayenne pepper, for sprinkling

MUSTARD TOASTS
125g softened butter
2 teaspoons Dijon mustard
3 cloves garlic, crushed
¼ cup finely chopped continental parsley
8 slices ciabatta or crusty bread

Place mussels in a large pot with ¼ cup water and simmer covered for 5-10 minutes until mussels open. Reserve 8 mussels in shells for garnish and remove the rest from their shells, straining any cooking liquid into the fish stock.

Heat oil in a pot and fry leek and celery until softened. Add butter and, when melted, stir in flour, cooking for 1 minute. Add fish stock all at once and bring to the boil, stirring until thickened. Add potatoes and simmer for 30 minutes until potatoes are tender. Return all mussels, including those in the shell, to the chowder. Add cream and cook until heated through. Season to taste. Serve portioned into bowls, distributing the mussels evenly. Sprinkle with cayenne and extra celery leaves. Serve with Mustard Toasts.

For **Mustard Toasts**, blend butter, mustard, parsley and garlic together. Spread mustard butter on both sides of the bread slices. Grill on both sides until golden. Serve with chowder.

TIPS
*To make your own fish stock, simmer fish bones with chopped carrot, celery, onion, bay leaf, peppercorns and a slice of lemon for 1 hour before straining.

STYLING
Use the mussels in the shell and little celery leaves to garnish the soup just before serving, as they will settle into the soup. Place a piece of toast at the bottom of the bowl to help support the mussels.

DRINK MATCH
Pinot grigio or Australian pale ale.

Main

Moroccan Chicken, Lentil and Spinach Soup with Coriander Oil

Serves 8 • **Preparation time** 15 minutes • **Cooking time** 1 hour

This is so much more than a soup - it's a tasty and nourishing meal. Slowly cooking the chicken in the soup flavours the stock, and the touch of Moroccan spice makes it deeply soul-warming.

1½ cups extra virgin olive oil
1 leek or large onion, sliced
3 stalks celery, diced
2-3 tablespoons ras el hanout (Moroccan spice mix)
1kg skinless chicken thighs
375g French-style green lentils, rinsed
2 litres water
sea salt, to taste
125g baby spinach leaves
2 tomatoes, finely diced
natural yoghurt, for serving
1 bunch coriander

Heat ½ cup oil in a large pot and sauté leek and celery over medium heat for 5 minutes until softened. Stir in ras el hanout and sauté until aromatic. Add chicken, lentils and water, and bring to the boil. Season to taste. Simmer covered for 45 minutes until chicken is tender.

Remove chicken from soup and shred, discarding the bones. Return shredded chicken to soup, add spinach leaves, and simmer until spinach has wilted. Season to taste.

Serve in bowls topped with chopped tomato, a dollop of yoghurt and drizzle of Coriander Oil.

For **Coriander Oil**, reserve some coriander leaves for garnish. Blend remaining chopped coriander and stalks with 1 cup olive oil using a handheld blender and season with salt.

VARIATION For a vegan-friendly version, use 500g sliced mushrooms in place of chicken and sauté when adding the spices. Simmer for 30 minutes only.

TIPS
French-style green lentils, known as puy lentils, are prized for their chewy texture and nutty flavour.

STYLING
Swirl the coriander oil on top of the soup after you have topped it with tomato.

DRINK MATCH
Pinot grigio, grenache or crisp lager.

WINTER COMFORTS

Main
Skillet Eggplant Parmigiana

Serves 2 • **Preparation time** 15 minutes • **Cooking time** 30 minutes

Perfect for two, this one-pan Sicilian-style eggplant parmigiana is a marvellous meat-free meal. I like to make it in a skillet that I can bring to the table.

1 large eggplant
¼ cup plain flour
olive oil, as needed
1 onion, finely diced
2 cloves garlic, crushed
400g can peeled tomatoes, chopped*
2 teaspoons chopped thyme or rosemary
sea salt and pepper, to taste
½ cup grated mozzarella cheese
2 tablespoons grated parmesan cheese
paprika, for sprinkling

Cut the eggplant lengthwise into 5mm thick slices and coat in flour. Heat 2 tablespoons oil in a skillet (use one that can be transferred to the oven) and fry a few slices of eggplant at a time until golden on both sides. Drain on absorbent paper. You may need to wipe out the skillet and add extra oil as you go.

Heat 1 tablespoon oil in the skillet and sauté the onion and garlic until softened. Add the tomatoes and thyme and simmer for 5 minutes until slightly thickened. Season to taste.

Arrange the eggplant slices into the sauce. Sprinkle with both cheeses and bake in the upper half of the oven at 200°C for 15-20 minutes until golden.

Sprinkle with extra thyme sprigs and paprika. Serve with crusty bread and salad.

VARIATION Also delicious made with chargrilled zucchini and capsicum.

TIPS
*Use scissors to chop peeled tomatoes while they are still in the can.

STYLING
Twist the eggplant slices as you add them to the dish so they sit up.

DRINK MATCH
Barbera, nebbiolo, or Italian pilsner.

My family's favourite Poulet au Pot...

Main
Poulet au Pot

Serves 4 • Preparation time 20 minutes • Cooking time 1 hour

This French classic 'Chicken-in-a-Pot' was a regular Sunday family feast as my kids were growing up. Whenever we gather and I bring it to the table, it still makes their hearts smile to this day!

¼ bunch continental parsley
1.8kg free-range chicken
sea salt and pepper, to taste
kitchen string
¼ cup pure olive oil
150g pancetta, prosciutto or bacon, chopped
8 baby onions, peeled or 1 leek, sliced
4 carrots, peeled and sliced
2 parsnips, peeled and sliced
2 stalks celery, sliced, and leaves
8 small potatoes, cut in half
4 cloves garlic, crushed
2 cups white wine
2 cups chicken stock
1 bay leaf
2 tablespoons butter, softened
2 tablespoons plain flour

Pick parsley leaves and chop stalks. Season chicken and tie legs together with kitchen string. Heat olive oil in a large flameproof casserole pot such as a French oven. Brown chicken on both sides until golden and remove.

In the same pot, sauté pancetta and onions until golden. Add carrots, parsnips, celery and leaves, potatoes and garlic, and sauté for 2 minutes.

Nestle chicken, breast side up, in the centre of the vegetables. Add wine, stock, bay leaf and parsley stalks and bring to the boil. Simmer covered for 30 minutes, then simmer uncovered for a further 20 minutes.

Mix butter and flour together to make a paste. Remove bay leaf. Bring casserole to the boil over high heat and whisk the butter mixture into the juices of the casserole until thickened.

Season to taste. Sprinkle with parsley and serve at the table with crusty bread.

VARIATION If there are any saucy leftovers, stir some peas and/or spinach leaves through it for another meal the next day.

TIPS
This can also be cooked in the oven instead of on the stovetop. Bake covered at 180°C for 30 minutes, then uncovered for 30 minutes.

STYLING
Spoon the thickened sauce over the chicken before sprinkling with parsley leaves and pepper and bringing to the table.

DRINK MATCH
Chardonnay or farmhouse ale

WINTER COMFORTS

Main
Seafood Chowder Pies

Makes 6 individual pies • **Preparation time** 20 minutes • **Cooking time** 20 minutes

Everyone loves a winter pie, and these hot little pots of creamy seafood with a crisp pastry top can also be made with just scallops or even chicken. They can be easily baked ahead of time and reheated as needed.

750g assorted seafood (prawns, scallops, salmon, white fish)
50g butter
1 leek, sliced
¼ cup plain flour
½ cup dry white wine
1 cup milk
½ cup grated vintage cheddar
½ cup corn kernels
1 teaspoon sea salt
black pepper, to taste
2 tablespoons chopped dill or parsley
3 sheets frozen puff pastry, thawed
1 egg, lightly beaten
sesame seeds, for sprinkling

Cut the seafood into bite-sized pieces.

Melt butter in a large pot and sauté leek on medium heat for 5-10 minutes until softened. Add flour and cook stirring for 1 minute. Add wine and milk and bring to the boil, stirring until thickened. Stir in the cheddar, seafood, corn, salt, pepper and dill. The seafood will not be cooked at this stage. Portion evenly into 6 x 1 cup ovenproof dishes.

Cut each sheet of pastry into 4 squares. Cover each dish with a pastry square and brush with lightly beaten egg. Cut the remaining squares diagonally into 4 triangles and use to decorate the top of the pies, overlapping them. Brush with egg and sprinkle with sesame seeds.

Bake at 200°C for 20 minutes until puffed and golden brown.

VARIATION Use 750g chopped chicken tenderloins in place of seafood and cook in the pan for a few minutes after sautéing the leek.

TIPS
This recipe can easily be made into one large family pie.

STYLING
Let the pastry overhang the dish for a rustic look.

DRINK MATCH
Chardonnay or Australian pale ale.

Main
Prosciutto and Porcini Beef Fillet

Serves 6 • **Preparation time** 20 minutes • **Cooking time** 20 minutes

Designed for my Christmas table one year, this recipe is a riff on Beef Wellington with the earthy flavour of porcini mushrooms. As the beef parcels can be wrapped ahead of time and roasted just prior to serving, they make sit-down entertaining for a crowd a breeze.

3 sheets frozen puff pastry, thawed
olive oil, as needed
6 x 200g thick beef fillet steaks
sea salt and pepper, to taste
fresh thyme sprigs
6 long slices prosciutto
1 punnet cherry tomatoes
2 tablespoons balsamic vinegar
50g butter
thyme, for garnish

PORCINI DUXELLES
20g dried porcini mushrooms
½ cup boiling water
150g Swiss brown mushrooms
1 tablespoon cognac or brandy
2 teaspoons fresh thyme

To make **Pastry Squares**, cut each pastry sheet in half and layer two pieces on top of each other - make 3 stacks. Cut each stack in half to make 6 squares and place on a baking tray. Score a 1cm border on each square and prick the bases with a fork. Bake at 220°C for 10 minutes until puffed and golden.

Season beef with salt and pepper. Heat oil in a heavy-based roasting pan on the stove and brown beef on both sides. Top each piece of beef with 1 tablespoon Porcini Duxelles, a sprig of thyme and wrap in a slice of prosciutto. Arrange tomatoes around beef and bake at 200°C for 10 minutes or until done to your liking. Remove beef and keep warm.

Deglaze pan with balsamic vinegar and reduce by half. Turn off heat and mix in butter to form a sauce. Serve beef on pastry squares with roasted tomatoes and drizzle with balsamic sauce. Garnish with thyme.

For the **Porcini Duxelles**, soak the porcini mushrooms in the boiling water for 10 minutes. Drain liquid into a large frypan and finely chop the soaked porcini and Swiss brown mushrooms together in a food processor. Add chopped mushrooms, cognac and thyme to the frypan and cook, stirring until liquid has reduced and the mixture is like a thick paste. Season well. Allow to cool and use as required.

TIPS
Cook pastry in advance and warm briefly in the oven while the meat rests and you are making the sauce.

STYLING
Create an assembly line when serving this dish so that you can present them identically.

DRINK MATCH
Cabernet Sauvignon, dark ale or West Coast IPA.

Main
Shiraz Beef Cheeks with Parsnip Pear Puree

Serves 6 • **Preparation time** 30 minutes • **Cooking time** 3 hours slow cooking

Winter means low and slow cooking of hearty meats, like these meltingly rich beef cheeks served over a creamy parsnip puree, with the surprising sweetness of winter pears.

1 leek
extra light olive oil, for frying
sea salt and pepper, to taste
1.2kg beef cheeks, trimmed
½ cup pure olive oil
2 stalks celery and leaves, diced
1 large carrot, peeled and diced
2 cloves garlic, crushed
2 ½ cups shiraz
12 pitted prunes
1 bay leaf
½ bunch fresh thyme, tied with string
baking paper
50g butter
½ cup toasted hazelnuts, halved

PARSNIP PEAR PUREE

1kg parsnips, peeled and chopped
2 pears, peeled
4 cloves garlic, peeled
2-3 cups chicken or vegetable stock
½ teaspoon salt
50g butter

To make crispy fried leeks, cut a 10cm length of the white part of the leek. Split along the length, peel into leaves and finely slice into strips. Reserve the strips for frying, and slice the rest of the leek for use in the casserole. Heat extra light olive oil and quickly fry strips of leek until golden. Drain on absorbent paper and use as a garnish.

Season beef cheeks. Heat ¼ cup olive oil in a large heavy-based casserole dish on the stove and brown beef on both sides. Remove. Add remaining oil and sauté sliced leek, celery, carrot and garlic for 5 minutes. Deglaze pan with shiraz. Return beef cheeks to pan with prunes, bay leaf and thyme and bring to the boil. Place a cartouche (piece of baking paper cut to fit the shape of the pot), directly on top of the beef cheeks. Cover and slow cook in the oven at 150°C for 2 ½-3 hours until very tender. Then simmer uncovered on stovetop for 5-10 minutes until sauce has reduced. Stir in butter. Serve over Parsnip Pear Puree, sprinkled with hazelnuts and crispy fried leek.

For the **Parsnip Pear Puree**, combine parsnips, pears, garlic, 2 cups stock and salt in a large saucepan and bring to the boil. Simmer covered for 15 minutes until very tender, adding more stock if needed. Puree and mix in butter.

TIPS
Add a few squares of dark chocolate for added depth of flavour.

STYLING
Position a little nest of crispy leeks on top of the dish.

DRINK MATCH
Shiraz, West Coast IPA or dry stout.

Main
Moroccan Tagine with Flatbreads

Serves 4-6 • **Preparation time** 15 minutes • **Cooking time** 20 minutes

The colours and aromas of roadside Moroccan eateries with fresh meat hanging in the wind, ready to be flamed in clay tagines, play in my head whenever I make this dish. It is also so versatile, it can be made with chicken, lamb or vegetables.

6 boneless chicken thighs or lamb loin chops, trimmed of fat
sea salt
2 tablespoons olive oil
1 onion, sliced
1 red capsicum, sliced
2-3 tablespoons ras el hanout*
2 teaspoons turmeric
1 tablespoon smoked paprika
2 cups water
750g butternut pumpkin, peeled and cut into 2cm cubes
2 carrots, peeled and sliced
400g can chickpeas, drained
grated rind of 1 lemon or ½ preserved lemon, diced
½ cup dried apricots or dates
½ bunch fresh coriander leaves
¼ cup toasted slivered almonds
natural yoghurt, for serving

FLATBREADS
250g bakers flour
200g fine semolina and extra for dusting
2 teaspoons sea salt
1⅓ cups warm water
2 teaspoons dried yeast

Season chicken with salt. Heat oil in a tagine or heavy-based casserole dish on the stove and lightly brown chicken on both sides. Add onion, capsicum and spices, and cook stirring until aromatic. Add water, pumpkin, carrots, chickpeas, lemon rind and apricots and simmer covered for 15 minutes until carrots are tender, adding extra water if needed. Simmer uncovered for 5 minutes to reduce slightly and season. Chop half the coriander and stir in. Sprinkle with almonds and remaining coriander and serve with natural yoghurt and Flatbreads.

For the **Flatbreads**, combine flour, semolina and salt in a bowl. Make a well in the centre, add the warm water to make a pool. Mix in yeast until dissolved then mix altogether by hand to form a dough. Turn out onto a floured surface and knead for 5-10 minutes, adding extra flour if needed, until smooth and elastic. Divide into 6 pieces. Dust the bench with semolina and roll out each into a 15 cm round. Dust each flatbread with semolina and stand for 15 minutes to rise slightly.

Cook flatbreads on an oiled flat griddle or non-stick pan for 3-5 minutes on each side until golden.

VARIATION Use ½ head cauliflower, cut into florets, in place of the meat and add with the pumpkin.

TIPS
*Ras el hanout is a Moroccan spice mix that translates as 'top of the shop', as spice vendors create their own blend of up to 100 spices.

STYLING
Spoon the tagine into a large serving bowl and garnish with a dollop of yoghurt, fresh coriander and paprika.

DRINK MATCH
Riesling or crisp lager.

Main
Mimi's Moussaka

Serves 6 • **Preparation time** 30 minutes • **Cooking time** 40 minutes

Moussaka is a delicious savoury bake that is a meal in itself. It can be prepared a day in advance before baking, and also reheats very well. This is my version that evolved from my mum's recipe. It doubles very well, so make two and freeze one! Serve with a fresh Greek salad.

1 large eggplant
sea salt and pepper, to taste
olive oil, as needed
4 potatoes, unpeeled
1 onion, finely chopped
1 clove garlic, crushed
500g lamb or beef mince
½ cup red or white wine
400g can peeled tomatoes
2 teaspoons beef stock powder
1 teaspoon Greek oregano
1 teaspoon cinnamon
¼ cup continental parsley, chopped
50g butter
¼ cup plain flour
2 cups milk
½ cup grated parmesan
⅓ cup dried panko breadcrumbs
¼ cup grated parmesan, extra
paprika, for sprinkling

Cut eggplant lengthwise into 1cm thick slices. Season with salt and allow to stand for 10 minutes. Heat 2 tablespoons olive oil in a large frypan and fry the eggplant until golden brown on both sides. Remove.

Cut potatoes into 1cm thick slices and place in the base of a lasagne dish. Drizzle with a little olive oil, season with salt and bake at 200°C for 15-20 minutes until tender.

Heat 2 tablespoons oil in frypan and sauté onion and garlic until softened. Add mince and brown well. Add wine, chopped tomatoes, stock powder, oregano, cinnamon and parsley, and season. Simmer for 10 minutes until thickened.

To make white sauce, melt butter in a saucepan. Add flour and cook stirring for 1 minute. Add milk all at once and bring to the boil, whisking until thickened. Stir in ½ cup parmesan.

To assemble Moussaka, layer potatoes with eggplant slices, mince, white sauce, breadcrumbs and extra parmesan. Sprinkle with paprika and drizzle with oil. Bake at 200°C for 30-40 minutes until golden brown. Serve cut into squares.

TIPS
Grill or chargill eggplants for a lighter Moussaka.

STYLING
Always let the moussaka stand for up to half an hour before cutting, so it cuts more easily into neat squares.

DRINK MATCH
Shiraz, tempranillo or amber ale.

WINTER COMFORTS

Main
Lamb Shank Navarin and Ploughman's Cheese Bread

It is the slow-simmered dishes of French cooking that beckon me every time. Here, lamb shanks get a French makeover to create a very heartwarming dish, served with an easy cheesy quick bread on the side. Perfect for fireside eating.

Lamb Shank Navarin

Serves 4 • **Preparation time** 30 minutes
Cooking time 2 hours

¼ cup plain flour
2 teaspoons paprika
sea salt and pepper, to taste
4 Frenched lamb shanks
olive oil, as needed
6 baby onions, peeled
4 stalks celery, sliced, and leaves
1 leek, sliced
1 cup red wine
400g can peeled tomatoes
1 litre beef stock
6 small new potatoes, unpeeled, halved
1 bouquet garni*
baking paper
1 bunch Dutch carrots, scrubbed and trimmed
200g baby turnips or 1 turnip, peeled and cut into wedges
½ cup frozen peas

Combine flour, paprika, 1 teaspoon salt and ¼ teaspoon pepper in a plastic bag. Add lamb shanks and toss to coat. Remove shanks and keep the flour. Heat 2 tablespoons oil in a large ovenproof casserole pot such as a French oven, then brown the onions and remove. Brown lamb shanks on all sides and remove. Wipe out the pot with absorbent paper.

Reserve the tender celery leaves. Add 2 tablespoons oil and sauté leek and celery over medium heat until softened. Add remaining flour and cook stirring for 1 minute. Add wine, tomatoes and stock and bring to the boil, breaking up the tomatoes with a spoon. Add potatoes and bouquet garni.

Place a cartouche (piece of baking paper cut to fit the shape of the pot) directly on top of the shanks. Cover and slow-cook in the oven at 160°C for 1 hour. Add carrots, turnips and onions and cook for 1 more hour until the lamb is very tender. Transfer to the stovetop and simmer uncovered for 10 minutes until slightly thickened. Mash some of the vegetables with a spoon to thicken the sauce further if desired.

Remove the bouquet garni. Stir in peas and celery leaves and simmer for 1 minute. Serve with **Ploughman's Cheese Bread**.

Ploughman's Cheese Bread

Serves 4 • **Preparation time** 5 minutes
Cooking time 25 minutes

2 cups self-raising flour
235g club cheddar cheese
   (pickled onion flavour or vintage)
1 tablespoon finely chopped fresh rosemary
1 cup milk
extra flour, as needed
extra milk, for brushing

Place flour into a large bowl and crumble cheese into flour with fingers until evenly distributed. Mix in rosemary.

Make a well in the centre of the flour. Add the milk and mix to a soft dough, adding a little extra flour if needed.

Turn out onto a floured surface and knead very lightly until just smooth.

Form into two logs, 5cm in diameter, and place on a floured baking tray. Brush with milk and bake at 180°C for 20-25 minutes or until golden brown. Allow to stand for 5 minutes before slicing.

TIPS
*Bouquet garni is a bundle of herbs, such as parsley, thyme, rosemary and bay leaf, tied together with kitchen string and used to flavour a dish. Remove before serving.

STYLING
Retain some celery leaves for a final garnish. When serving, spoon the large pieces of food onto the plate, then arrange the smaller bits and sauce around them.

DRINK MATCH
Shiraz or red ale.

WINTER COMFORTS

Main

Rosemary Beef Short Ribs with Sweet Pea Puree

Serves 4-6 • **Preparation time** 20 minutes • **Cooking time** 2 ½ hours

When a friend asked me for a short rib recipe, I was inspired to dig mine out and revamp it with a contrasting sweet pea puree to give it a bright touch. Ask the butcher for asado short ribs for best results.

1.5kg beef asado short ribs
sea salt and pepper, to taste
2 tablespoons olive oil
1 large red onion, cut into wedges
4 large cloves garlic, chopped
1 cup red wine
1 cup beef stock
1 tablespoon dark brown sugar
1 tablespoon seeded mustard
1 bunch rosemary
50g softened butter

SWEET PEA PUREE
60g butter
2 large cloves garlic, chopped
3 cups frozen baby peas
1 cup chicken stock

Cut short ribs into pieces between the bones and season. Heat oil in a large heavy-based ovenproof pot such as a French oven, and brown ribs on all sides. Add onions and garlic and sauté until softened. Add wine, stock, sugar, mustard and 4 long sprigs of rosemary, and bring to the boil.

Cover and bake at 160°C for 2 hours until meat is tender. Remove ribs and keep warm. Simmer pan juices until syrupy and season. Turn off the heat and stir in butter to make a sauce.

Serve ribs on a pool of Sweet Pea Puree. Spoon sauce on top and garnish with fresh rosemary.

For the **Sweet Pea Puree,** melt 50g butter in a saucepan and sauté garlic until softened. Add peas and stock. Bring to the boil and simmer covered for 10 minutes. Puree in a blender with remaining 10g butter until smooth. Season and serve with short ribs.

VARIATION Also delicious with sweet potato mash instead of the pea puree.

TIPS
Asado beef ribs are cut across the rib for extra flavour.

STYLING
Spoon pea puree on the base of a flat bowl, top with three ribs, spoon sauce over and finish with rosemary sprigs and pepper.

DRINK MATCH
Cabernet sauvignon, shiraz, West Coast IPA or red ale.

Main
Surprise Mozzarella Meatballs

Serves 4 • **Preparation time** 15 minutes • **Cooking time** 20 minutes

My mate Mandy's aunty is the original source of this recipe that I have tweaked a bit over the years, so thanks to her! I love how a recipe shared becomes a recipe loved. This has definitely become a firm family favourite and my grown-up kids still love it. Make double so you can make Italian meatball subs for lunch.

- 200g block mozzarella or cheddar cheese
- 500g pork and veal mince
- 1 small onion, grated
- 1 small carrot, peeled and grated
- 1 cup fresh breadcrumbs
- 1 egg
- 2 tablespoons chopped continental parsley
- sea salt and pepper, to taste
- 750ml tomato passata
- 1 cup red wine
- 2 tablespoons extra virgin olive oil
- continental parsley leaves, for garnish

Cut cheese into 12 cubes. Combine mince, onion, carrot, breadcrumbs, egg, parsley, 1 teaspoon salt and ½ teaspoon pepper together until well combined. Form mixture into twelve meatballs, inserting a cube of cheese into the centre of each.

Simmer tomato passata, wine and oil together in a large pot and season to taste. Add meatballs and simmer covered for 15-20 minutes until cooked through.

Sprinkle with pepper and extra parsley and serve with crusty bread, pasta, mash or rice.

VARIATION Stuffed green olives can be used in place of the cheese for a non-dairy 'surprise' centre.

TIPS
Be sure to use a good quality natural Italian-style passata with no additives for a really authentic flavour.

STYLING
Serve a few meatballs on a pool of sauce in a pasta bowl with shavings of parmesan cheese and parsley on top.

DRINK MATCH
Sangiovese or Italian pilsner.

WINTER COMFORTS

Main

Bourbon Beef Brisket with Quickles and Celeriac Slaw

I know from my US travels that real American barbecue is absolutely mouthwatering, but my cheat's version of this smoky brisket will surprise and delight because of how easy it is to make and how good it tastes. The celeriac slaw is a bright and fresh side dish that also happens to be fructose-free.

Smoky Bourbon Beef Brisket

Serves 6 • **Preparation time** 10 minutes
Cooking time 4 hours

2kg whole piece of beef brisket
sea salt and pepper, to taste
1 tablespoon olive oil
2 large red onions, sliced
4 cloves garlic, crushed
1 tablespoon smoked paprika
1 cup bourbon
1 cup smoky barbecue sauce

Season beef. Heat oil in a heavy-based ovenproof pot and brown on one side until golden. Turn over, add onions and garlic, sautéing as the meat browns on the second side.

Add smoked paprika and sauté until aromatic. Add bourbon and barbecue sauce. Cover and bake at 150°C for 4 hours until the beef is very tender.

Remove beef and allow to rest while simmering the sauce on the cooktop for 5 minutes until reduced. Serve sliced brisket and sauce with Celeriac Slaw and Quickles.

For **Quickles**, combine 1 sliced red onion, 4 sliced pickled cucumbers, 2 tablespoons red wine vinegar, 1 tablespoon sugar and 1 teaspoon salt together and stand for 10 minutes.

Celeriac, Almond and Caraway Slaw

Serves 6 • **Preparation time** 20 minutes

500g celeriac
grated rind and juice of 1 large lemon
1 large carrot, peeled and grated
½ cup chopped coriander or parsley leaves
¼ cup egg mayonnaise or sour cream
1 tablespoon Dijon mustard
2 teaspoons caraway or fennel seeds
1 teaspoon salt
1 teaspoon sugar
2 tablespoons toasted slivered almonds

Peel celeriac and cut into matchstick strips with a mandolin, or use a grater. Immediately pour boiling water over celeriac. Allow to stand for 1 minute, then rinse under cold running water and drain well.

Combine with remaining ingredients, adding almonds just before serving to maintain their crunch.

Season and serve garnished with coriander leaves.

196　　　　　　　　　　　　　　　　　　　　　　　　　　　TASTE*ful*

Main
Rigatoni with Italian Sausage and Spinach Ragù

Serves 4 • **Preparation time** 10 minutes • **Cooking time** 30 minutes

A plate of pasta is surely the most comforting of dishes. Using homestyle Italian pork sausages to make the sauce absolutely packs it with flavour in a very short amount of time. The good slug of red wine helps a bit too. Buon Appetito!

extra virgin olive oil as needed
1 large onion, chopped
4 cloves garlic, chopped
500g Italian pork sausages, sliced
1 cup dry red wine
750ml tomato passata
sea salt and pepper, to taste
80g spinach leaves
500g rigatoni pasta
shaved parmesan cheese, for serving

Heat 1 tablespoon oil in a large pot and sauté onion and garlic until softened. Add sausages and cook, stirring until well-browned.

Add wine and passata and bring to the boil. Simmer for 20 minutes until reduced and thickened. Stir in 2 tablespoons oil and spinach and season to taste, stirring until spinach wilts.

Meanwhile, cook pasta in a large pot of salted boiling water until al dente. Drain and toss through sauce. Serve sprinkled with cheese.

VARIATION Fresh basil leaves or rocket can be used in place of spinach.

TIPS
Make double the ragù and freeze for pasta emergencies!

STYLING
Shave parmesan with a vegetable peeler.

DRINK MATCH
Sangiovese, shiraz or Italian pilsner.

Main

Slow-cooked Pork, Spinach and Cannellini Bean Pot Roast with Salt-roasted Chats

Serves 4-6 • **Preparation time** 15 minutes • **Cooking time** 2 ½ hours

This Italian-syle pot roast of succulent slow-cooked pork neck with creamy cannellini beans is a hearty winter warmer. Serve it with salt-roasted chat potatoes.

- 1.5kg pork neck (or trimmed loin of pork)
- sea salt and pepper, to taste
- ¼ cup pure olive oil
- 1 onion, finely chopped
- 3 cloves garlic, crushed
- 1 large stalk celery and leaves, chopped
- 1 cup dry white wine
- 400g can peeled tomatoes
- 400g can cannellini beans, drained and rinsed
- 1 bunch fresh sage leaves
- 100g baby spinach leaves
- 2 tablespoons extra virgin olive oil
- 1kg baby potatoes, unpeeled

Season pork with pepper. Heat olive oil in a heavy-based casserole dish and brown pork on all sides.

Arrange onion, garlic and celery around the meat and sauté for 2 minutes. Add wine, tomatoes and beans, cover and bring to the simmer. Bake covered at 150°C for 2 hours until pork is soft. Remove pork and rest covered in foil.

Meanwhile, add 2 tablespoons sage leaves to pan juices and boil down until reduced by half. Season to taste and mix in spinach leaves, stirring until wilted. Stir in extra virgin olive oil. Carve pork into slices, spoon over sauce and garnish with sage. Serve with Salt Roasted Chats.

For **Salt Roasted Chats**, wash but do not dry. Cut a cross in the top of potatoes and dip the tops into sea salt. The potatoes should be slightly wet so the salt sticks.

Roast at 200°C for 30 minutes until golden brown, or alternatively, roast in the oven with the pork at 150°C until they are tender, and then, once the pork is cooked, roast at 220°C for 5-10 minutes to crisp the potatoes.

TIPS
Pork neck is sometimes sold as pork scotch fillet or pulled pork. Check with your butcher.

STYLING
Spoon some sauce onto a large platter. Top with sliced pork and more sauce and garnish with sage leaves.

DRINK MATCH
Chardonnay, pinot noir or cloudy apple cider.

WINTER COMFORTS

Main

Giant Pumpkin and Bacon Pie

Serves 6-8 • **Preparation time** 30 minutes • **Cooking time** 30 minutes

This olive oil pastry is a cinch to make and roll out, and once you have learned how to make it you can change up the filling to make any type of pie you like. This giant pie is particularly magnificent when brought to the table whole, then cut into wedges for sharing.

3 cups plain flour
1 teaspoon salt
⅔ cup warm water
½ cup extra virgin olive oil
2 tablespoons pure olive oil
1 leek, finely sliced
4 rashers bacon, sliced
700g peeled pumpkin, grated
1 tablespoon fresh rosemary leaves
200g smoked or vintage cheddar cheese, grated
sea salt and pepper, to taste
1 egg, lightly beaten
2 teaspoons caraway or fennel seeds

Combine flour and salt in a bowl. Make a well in the centre and mix in water and extra virgin olive oil to make a smooth dough. Do not overknead. Wrap in plastic wrap and allow to rest while making the filling.

Heat olive oil in a large frypan and sauté leek and bacon over medium heat for 5 minutes until softened. Add pumpkin and sauté a further 2 minutes until just softened. Allow mixture to cool, then stir in rosemary and cheese and season to taste.

Cut pastry dough in half and thinly roll out one piece to fit a 30cm pizza tray, rolling it slightly larger than the tray. Place pastry on tray, brush with egg and top with pumpkin filling. Thinly roll out remaining pastry and use to cover the filling. Pinch edges of pastry together to seal. Brush with egg and sprinkle with caraway seeds.

Bake at 220°C in the centre of the oven for 15 minutes, and then lower to the base of the oven for a further 10-15 minutes until golden brown underneath.

VARIATION Use grated mixed vegetables or wilted spinach in place of pumpkin.

TIPS
Pie can be assembled up to 2 hours before cooking and will freeze well once cooked.

STYLING
Pleat the edges of the pie as you would an empanada, pinching and folding as you go.

DRINK MATCH
Chardonnay, riesling, pinot noir, West Coast IPA or pumpkin ale.

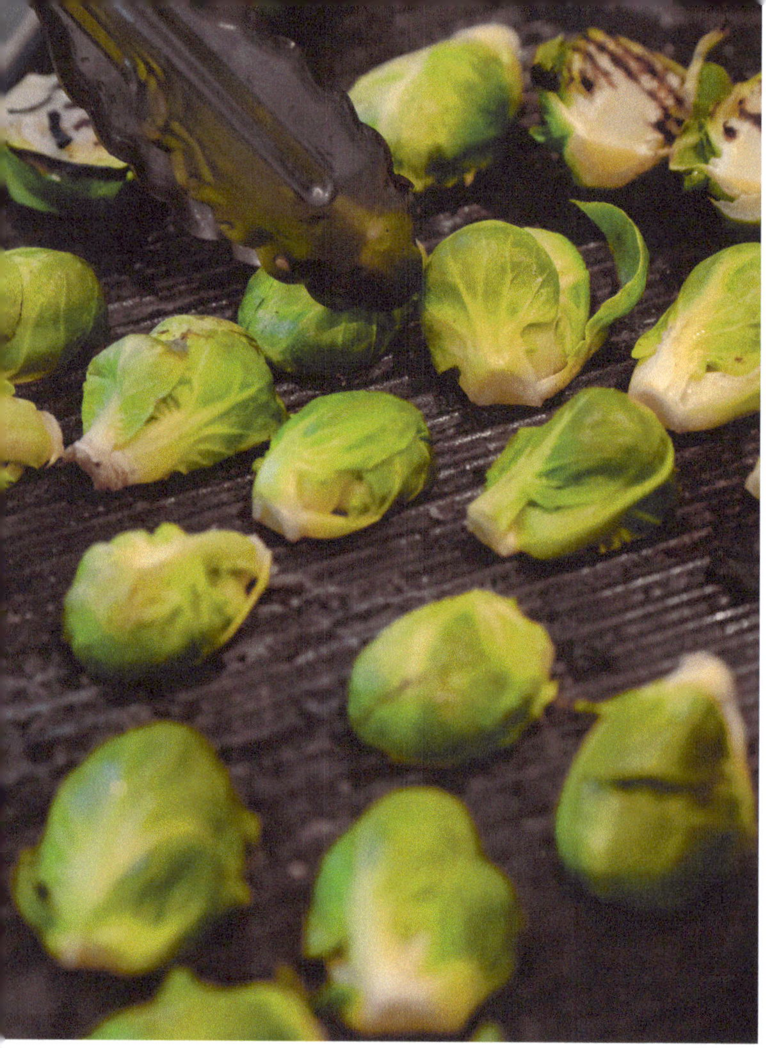
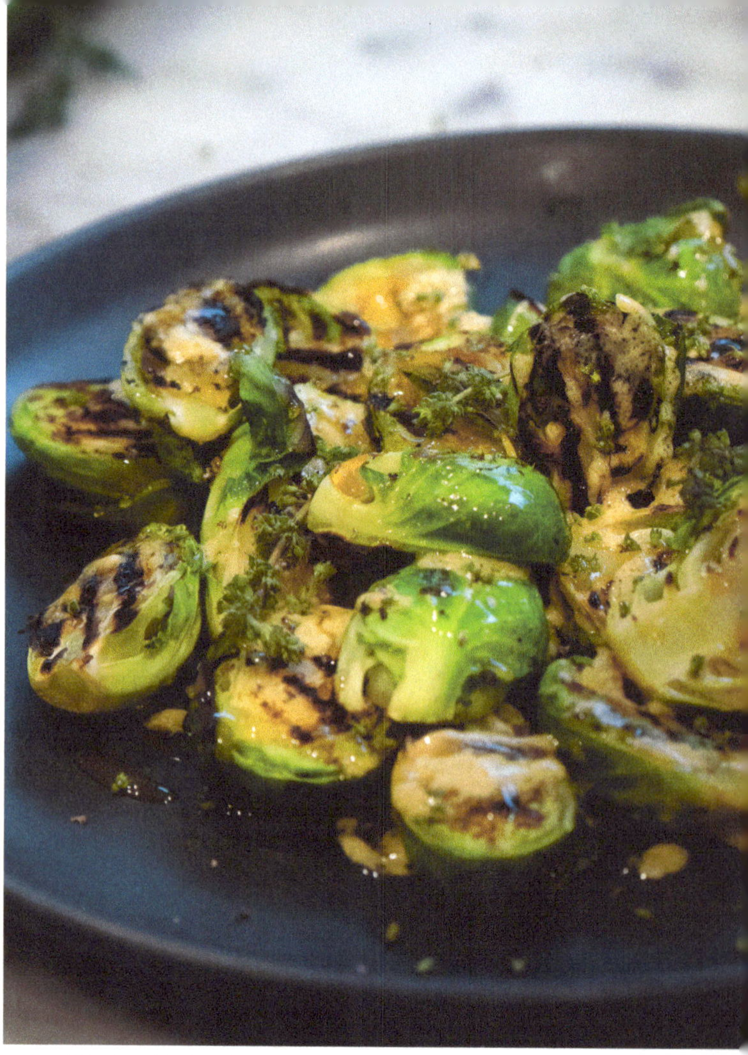
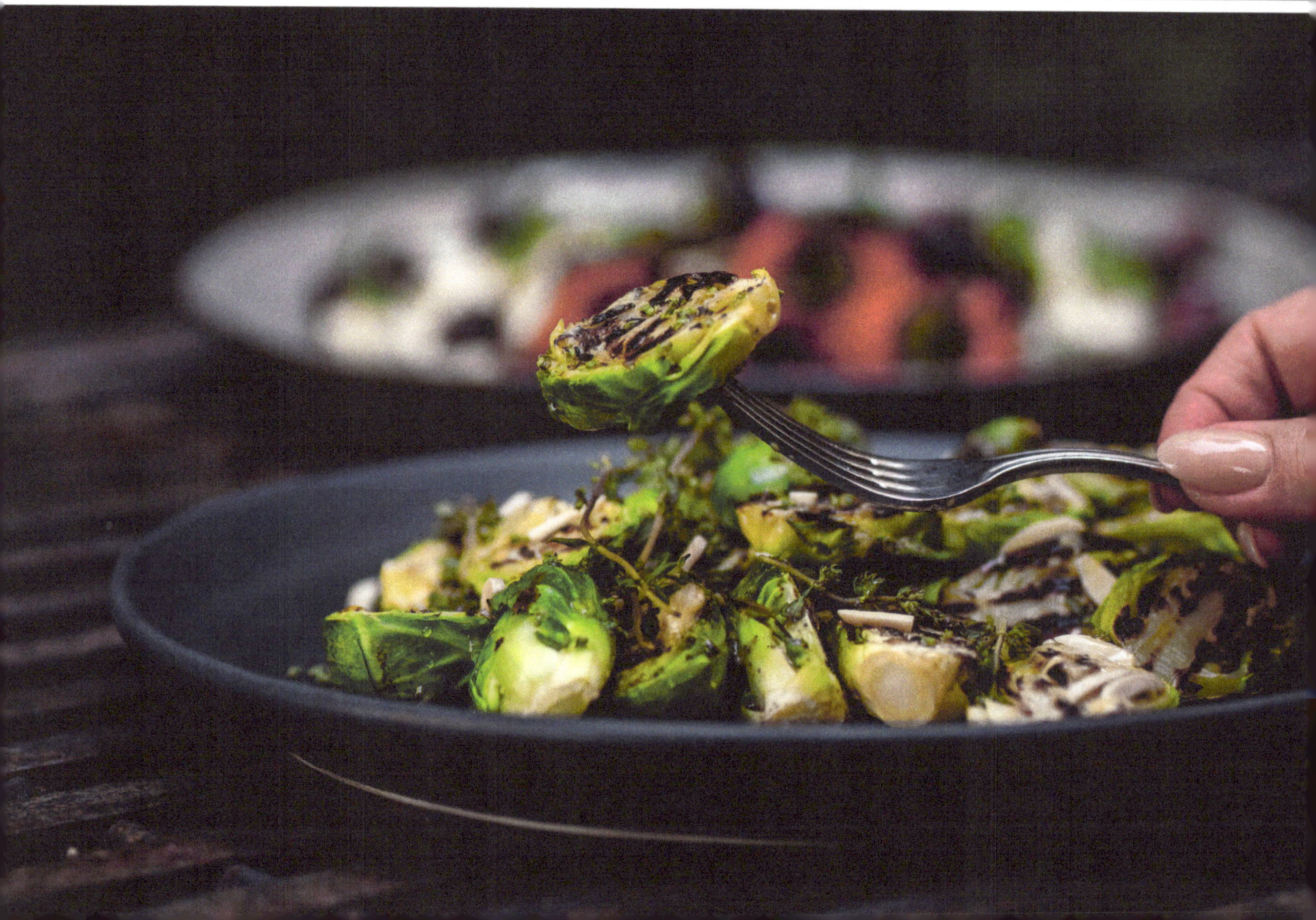

Side

Honeyed Brussels Sprouts with Almond and Dijon Dressing

Serves 4 • **Preparation time** 10 minutes • **Cooking time** 15 minutes

A much-maligned vegetable, the secret to tasty brussels sprouts is to caramelise them until they're golden, stopping when they are just tender and still bright green. A drizzle of honey makes them shine, and a sprinkle of toasted nuts never goes astray.

500g brussels sprouts
sea salt and pepper, to taste
honey, for drizzling
1 tablespoon toasted slivered almonds
fresh thyme, for sprinkling
curry powder, for sprinkling (optional)

DIJON DRESSING
1 tablespoon Dijon mustard
2 tablespoons lemon juice
¼ cup extra virgin olive oil

Cut brussels sprouts in half. Chargrill on both sides until charred and just tender, but still bright green.

Arrange on a platter. Season and drizzle with Dijon Dressing and honey. Sprinkle with almonds, fresh thyme and a little curry powder.

For the **Dijon Dressing**, shake all ingredients together in a jar to make a dressing.

VARIATION The dressing works well with charred asparagus or zucchini too.

TIPS
Dijon dressing will keep refrigerated in a jar for a few weeks, so make double!

STYLING
Tumble charred brussels sprouts on the plate with some cut surfaces up and some down, before dressing and finishing with a sprinkling of curry powder and thyme.

DRINK MATCH
Sauvignon blanc, riesling or crisp lager.

Big thanks and love

It has been a journey of a lifetime to get to the creation of this cookbook and it is a joy to have brought it to fruition with lots of help and inspiration along the way.

Firstly, thanks go to Josh Lynott, whose beautiful photography captured every moment perfectly, and the talented Jacqui Porter, who instantly understood my style and interpreted it into the elegant design.

To Susan Dean, Natalie Deane, Izzy Smith, Jazmine Morales and the team at Dean Publishing, for helping to steer me through the publishing process with gentle care and enthusiasm.

To my mentors, peers and colleagues from my early days as a young home economist and food stylist, to my time as a marketing manager. I thank you for the guidance, growth, inspiration and faith you have given me, both professionally and personally, over the course of my career - Ann Creber, Janet Lillie, the teams at the Gas Cookery Service, Australian Dairy Corporation and Dairy Australia Test Kitchens, Melanie Ryan, Lisa O'Shannessy, Bianca Stafrace, Julie Monaghan, Amanda Menegazzo, Pam Tannourji, Patricia Colaci, Paula Papas, Stuart Nicolson, Peter Singline, Nikki Adamo, Anneka Manning, Catherine Saxelby and Louis Petruccelli.

To my friend Gabriel Gaté, who I first cooked with on Channel 9's *What's Cooking?* decades ago, and have had many touch points with throughout the years. He is a shining example of a great food educator and I thank him for his contagious optimism, encouragement and kind words.

To Amber Phillips for the wonderful stay and allowing us to photograph at the gorgeous Flinders Beach Shack.

To my regular Cook-Along crew who have Zoomed into my kitchen every week over the past two years. We continue to learn, cook, laugh and share many of these recipes together, and the feedback from them and their families has been invaluable.

To the Pizza Party pals who came along to enjoy the pizzas from my kitchen that were expertly cooked by Dom on our charcoal barbie, and be photographed in the process - Dylan, Matt, Lucy, Tom, Mekeally, Marcus, Kendall and, of course, Josh!

To the countless friends and relatives who have cooked with me in my kitchen and shared so many unforgettable happy times at my table that have bonded us for life and to those who continue to inspire me with their zest for living - Fabio Robles, Eleni Spataro, Caterina Intemerato, Wendy Hirst, Liz Pearse and Natasha Eracleous.

To my dear dad, who left us much too soon, but in that time, impressed upon me the love of continuous learning, the value of art and creativity, and how to fully appreciate when magic moments happen.

To my generous and fearless mum, for being my first cooking teacher and for instilling in me the joy of gathering people to the table with true *philoxenia*, and to my darling sister, Aliki, her family and my in-laws for their steadfast support and many memorable meals together.

Most importantly, to my own little family, Domenic, Jordan and Talia and their partners, Laura and Ben, who supported and believed in me with the purest form of love, are always enthusiastic cohorts in my food adventures and are my favourite people to feed.

I am forever grateful.

Naomi
x

(*Philoxenia* is the Greek word that translates as 'friend to the stranger' but its meaning is more about an eagerness to show hospitality that is such an intrinsic part of Greek culture).

When Naomi met Josh

Josh breezed into my kitchen one day when he came for a visit with a dear friend. This sun-bronzed free spirit with the sunshine smile and I quickly hit it off when we started to talk about running events and photography.

He had never photographed food before, so we decided to have a play one day during his stay to see what would transpire. What evolved was a unique alchemy between our very diverse experiences, producing emotive images that truly captured the moment and the generous spirit of my food.

So, we decided to create this cookbook, an item on my wish list that I had put off for many years. Josh's 'Why Don't You?'* attitude and energetic presence inspired me to finally get this project off the ground.

We took most of the year to photograph the book in line with the seasons, in and around my home and favourite family holiday spots. Josh would fly in from the Gold Coast every couple of months with his backpack full to the brim, and move in for the duration of the shoot. I would cook, he would shoot and we would eat!

I love Josh's keen eye and the new perspective he brings to every dish I place before his camera. It's like my food takes on a new life through his eyes, and all the love and care that has gone into it seems to shine through on the plate.

About Naomi

Naomi's life has always revolved around food – selecting, cooking and celebrating with it.

As an award-winning food educator, television presenter, stylist and food writer with more than 35 years' experience in Australia's food industry, she has the wonderful job of creating something every day. Whether it is a new recipe, a beautiful image or some inspiring words on a page, it is always centred around food, a thing that sustains, nurtures and excites.

Her inspiring recipe ideas keep the home cook in mind, making it easy for everyone to produce mouth-watering meals in their own kitchen. Although her food style is grounded in her Mediterranean heritage, she has strong knowledge of the cuisines of Europe, the Middle East and South America, due to her extensive food travels, research and culinary experiences. Her career as a test kitchen manager and marketing manager, and now Director of Naomi Crisante Food Communications and Founder of foodcentric.com.au, has given her a broad suite of expertise in communications, consumer advisory, recipe development, masterclasses, event management and presentations. She has authored two commercial cookbooks (*Cheese Matters* and *Crowd Pleasers*), is an accredited cheese judge and has appeared regularly on many Australian cooking TV programs over the years.

Her food site, foodcentric.com.au, is a hub of food inspiration with a regular food blog, email newsletter, live recipe database, podcasts, travelogues, videos and an active social media following. She also runs virtual consumer cooking classes online and hands-on team cooking classes for corporate clients, both here and overseas.

To Naomi, being foodcentric is more than just an idea, it's a way of life…

Instagram @food.centric

About Josh

From when he took his first photo at eight years of age, Josh has been dedicated to finding a connection between him and the rest of the world through photography.

His positive and adventurous spirit has led him on a global quest to discover what it means to truly connect, with the aim to impart all that is positive in his life into the lives of others.

His outgoing personality and zest for life shows in every photo, inspiring his family and friends.

With the hope of impacting a worldwide audience, he is driven to bring inspirational thoughts through his photography and writing to as many people as possible on a daily basis.

Instagram @joshlynott

Why Don't You? Thoughts Worth Thinking by Joshua Lynott is Josh's first book, filled with his mesmerising photographs and thought-provoking words.

First published in 2022 by Naomi Crisante Food Communications

Text Copyright © Naomi Crisante 2022
The moral right of the author has been asserted.
Photography© Joshua Lynott 2022

Creative direction: Jacqui Porter, northwoodgreen.com
Editing: Dean Publishing
Food styling: Naomi Crisante
Food Assistants: Melanie Ryan, Patricia Colaci, Bianca Stafrace, Maria Penido
Wine and Beer Matches: Jordan Crisante, Naomi Crisante
Special thanks: Domenic Crisante, Talia Crisante, Gabriel Gaté, Amanda Menegazzo, Julie Monaghan

Disclaimer: While care has been taken to ensure the information is true and correct at the time of publication, changes in circumstances after the time of publication may impact on the accuracy of information. The author gives no warranty or assurance, and makes no representation to the accuracy or reliability of information for the intended use.

All rights reserved. No part of this publication may be reproduced, stored in a retrieval system or transmitted in any form by any means, electronic, mechanical, photocopying, recording or otherwise, without the prior written permission of the publishers and copyright holders.

ISBN 978 1 925452 57 0

Scan the QR codes below to access Naomi's curated playlists that match each chapter.

Spring Flings

Summer Love

Autumn Passions

Winter Comforts

www.ingramcontent.com/pod-product-compliance
Lightning Source LLC
Chambersburg PA
CBHW041509220426
43661CB00017B/1289